The
JESHUA LETTERS

Dedicated

to

the One

we all are

The
JESHUA LETTERS

Jayem with Jeshua

The Jeshua Letters

Fifth Edition

WAY *of* MASTERS
www.wayofmastery.com

Published by:
PT. Heartfelt Publishing
PO Box 204, Ubud 80571
admin@wayofmastery.com
www.wayofmastery.com

ISBN: 978-602-9189-19-3
© 1991 Jayem
1st Edition 1995
2nd Edition 2006
3rd Edition (Heartfelt Publishing) 2011
4th Edition (Heartfelt Publishing) 2013
5th Edition (Heartfelt Publishing) 2021
only authorized versions

Jeshua Shares

I promise you this: If you become *wholly committed* to awakening from the dream you have dreamed since the stars first began to appear in the heavens, and even before that, if your one desire is to be only what God created . . . then lay at the altar of your heart with every breath, everything you *think* you know, everything you *think* you need, and look lovingly upon every place that fear has made a home in your mind, and allow correction to come. It will come. Regardless of how you experience it, it *will* come.

And the day and the moment will arise when all of your pain and fear and suffering will have vanished like a wind that pushes the foam of the wave away, revealing the clarity of the ocean beneath you. You will literally feel throughout your being that there never was a dream. Some memories will remain with you and you will know that somewhere you must've dreamed a dream or had a thought of wondering what it would be like to be other than the way God created you, but it will be such a faint echo that it will leave no trace upon you. In your heart you will smile gently, regardless of the circumstances in which you find yourself. There will be peace from the crown of the head to the tips of the toes, so to speak, and that peace will walk before you wherever you go. It will enter a room before you enter it with a body, and those who are becoming sensitive will wonder who has come into their place. And some will even say, "Behold, I believe Christ has come for dinner." And you will be that one, for that is who you are—Christ eternal.

~ The Early Years: Choose to See

Contents

Acknowledgements

It is a joy to express my heartfelt gratitude for all those who have helped make this newly revised 5th edition of The Jeshua Letters available to you. First, my gratitude to author and teacher, Alan Cohen, who recognized the significance of the book and both encouraged me to publish it and, in prophetic accord with Jeshua, offered to write the original foreword; the late Joan Reddish, whose financial support miraculously made publication of the original edition possible; Sara Patton for manuscript preparation; Sandy Button, who left a secure corporate job to land here in Bali and, beginning in 2006, has been a tireless administrative helpmate for all facets of my work – from managing Alam Cinta Ashram in Ubud, to virtually every creation flowering from the development of The Way of Mastery Pathway – I can't imagine how it all could have occurred without her.

To all the many students from around the world that have dived deep with me into the alchemy of genuine spiritual transformation, your flowering souls are proof to me of the power of Love.

Lastly, and eternally, to my friend Jeshua ben Joseph, unseen yet ever present, whose love has healed my heart and who has kept an ancient promise, delivering me Home, guiding me into the depth of truly understanding the dynamics of separation and the Way of enlightenment and how to convey it usefully to others. From my humble beginnings as a doubting, reluctant, scared, and wounded man of thirty-seven, to this present being of seventy, who could not have imagined where He was leading me, I am fulfilled, at peace, and having a ball helping others heal and awaken into the extraordinary, ordinary life of Christ Mind. His love and guidance is the inspiration for my work and life; I shall never be able to say "thank you" enough.

A Note For The Reader

You will note that my name in this book is 'Marc.' For the past several years, it has been 'Jon Marc.' My friends call me 'Jayem,' which is the name I prefer, just for its simplicity!

Why the change?

As a child, and through much of my adult life, my name was 'Marc.' However, I always felt – even when very young – that the name was somehow incorrect, and that my name should be 'Jon' (and no 'h,' please!).

In the mid '90s, as a result of exploring in depth what is commonly called the 'shadow,' including intensive birth and womb healing work, I added 'Jon.' The result was an immediate and strong visceral shift, a movement into a deeper sense of wholeness.

When I announced this to my mother, she shared – after she lifted her jaw from the floor – that the names originally chosen for me and my identical twin brother were 'Jon' and 'Marc.' My brother died three days before my birth by emergency cesarean. In all the confusion, the names were changed; 'Marc' was ascribed to me, while 'Martin Jon' was given to my brother.

It seems that from my time in the womb, I knew my real name!

However, it has always seemed appropriate to remain faithful to the use of 'Marc' in The Jeshua Letters, especially because no words uttered herein by Jeshua have ever been edited or altered whatsoever. What you read is exactly what He said to me.

I would also like to point out – especially to former readers of the original edition – there is some expansion here, revealing more of what I experienced during these first few years with Jeshua. Originally, much material was withheld at Jeshua's request; what is added here is also by His guidance. I can only assume it is timely.

Foreword

This 5th edition of *The Jeshua Letters* shares the story of my initial encounter, and subsequent communion, with Jeshua ben Joseph (Jesus). But more than a mere recounting, it is the first building block in His extraordinary purpose of restoring His original teachings and building a pathway devoted to guiding us into the profound enlightenment and mastery that He calls 'Christ Mind.'

Though I had no awareness of His plan, in time, He would bring forth *The Way of the Servant* and the brilliant *Christ Mind Trilogy* – a three-year course given 'live' as recorded audio and later transcribed as three interconnected books: *The Way of the Heart*, *The Way of Transformation*, and *The Way of Knowing*. Together, these are the five essential, core texts of *The Way of Mastery Pathway*, given in the order they were first created. Each text is equally important. In *The Jeshua Letters*, He gives us the truth about reality and the Self, establishing the cornerstone for all that will follow. Then, in *The Way of the Servant*, He describes and transmits the living energy of the very goal of spirituality, the highest and final stage we can realize in this world. These two books set the stage for immersion in the living journey of *The Christ Mind Trilogy*.

During and immediately after scribing *The Jeshua Letters* and *The Way of the Servant,* there was a several-year process in which Jeshua adapted my body and mind – He essentially displaced my consciousness with his own, so he could teach 'live' to groups all over the U.S. These sessions have been collected and transcribed as *The Early Years*, which cover a wide range of fascinating subjects (His life, the soul, sexuality, and much more). Further along the rich unfolding of His *Pathway* came *The Living Practices* and *The Aramaic Teachings*, which I have come to view as the 'graduate school' of *The Pathway*.

All the elements of *The Pathway* have been brought forth through my continued communication with Jeshua – over decades – from His direct guidance and at His request. Yet, all that matters, dear reader, is that you are holding this specific volume, now. What if

God's Love is already answering the deepest prayer of your heart's longing, offering you what is most helpful? It is the quality of our 'studentship' and depth of our willingness to open and receive that are the critical essence of the journey!

In my own journey, I marvel as I reflect on all that has followed since His first appearance to me in July 1987, out of a field of brilliant white and golden light. Jeshua's apparition was full bodied, as if I were speaking to another human being standing right in front of me, in my living room! The events of that day would profoundly, utterly, and radically change the course of my entire life, as it would for thousands of others.

He appeared as I sat in open-eyed meditation, having responded to a Voice that vibrated within me, as well as all around, asking me to 'sit and meditate.' Afterwards, and for the next few days, all background mental chatter completely stopped. There was a lucid stillness, and though I continued to function in great effortlessness, I sensed a profound shift as if moved from one sphere of 'my life' into a new sphere of 'I am only now beginning to discover real life,' as if the bell had rung, and recess was over! Immediately following the completion of *The Jeshua Letters*, just minutes after the 'ink was dry,' I was guided to write the following:

> A moment ago, as I completed the last sentence of this book, a memory flashed suddenly across my mind. It came with such clarity and power that I not only saw the image, but I also experienced the smells and sensations.

> I am about five years of age, and my mother has brought me to an evening service at church. There are candles in every windowsill, their enchanting light flickering off stained glass that seems to disappear far above me into pointed arches.

> We sit in hard wooden pews that – from my viewpoint – stretch on for an enormous distance, finally giving way to a carpeted platform, upon which sits an altar draped in fine white linen edged with a golden fringe. On the altar are two

candelabras placed on either side of a golden crucifix.

Beyond the altar hangs a towering cross that reaches from the vaulted ceiling all the way down to the altar itself.

I feel something. Turning to my mother, I state matter-of-factly, "He is here, Mommy."

Without turning her head from the hymn book she is thumbing through, she asks, "Who is here, dear?"

"Christ," I answer confidently.

Now she turns to look at me. "No, honey, that is not Christ. That is the minister you see."

I cannot see the minister at all. "No, Mommy, Christ is here!" My response is insistent, and somewhat loud, so that the man sitting on the other side of my mother glances at me, then at my mother. Both of them smile and I am asked to be quiet, as the service is about to begin.

With surprise, it becomes clear that no one else has noticed Him and, perhaps for the first time, I doubt. But what, then, was that feeling?

Later, when I had learned to read, I would often sneak a flashlight to bed and, when I was sure everyone else was asleep, I would get out my Bible, crawl way down in the covers to shield the light, and grapple with the discrepancy between the feeling I got from the words attributed to Jesus (the same feeling I had in church that night) and what everyone else was telling me His words meant. I even prayed a lot, since I had been taught that God answers prayers. I was pretty sure my requests had been overlooked!

Gradually I grew frustrated. The older I got, the more I realized I was in the minority. In fact, as my social world expanded, it seemed apparent that most people really didn't care much about such things. They were either too busy to think about it, or they were quite sure where Christ was: in heaven, sitting at the right hand of God.

I don't remember just when it happened, but I came to forget that feeling and in my own way became entranced with the drama of my life, just like everyone else.

But the Question never really died. It resurfaced years later and led me to an intensive study of philosophy and comparative religion, where I discovered the treasures of the East: the sublime wisdom of Zen and especially the deep insights and transformative ways of yoga and meditation. Here, that feeling seemed to be not only understood, but actually sought and refined!

For all my enthusiasm and periods of discipline, I also spent a great deal of time avoiding the subject, distracting myself with the conventional forms of avoidance with which we are all familiar. Still, my fondness for Eastern spirituality continued and, over the years, I moved farther and farther away from anything having to do with Christianity. It is that simple fact that makes receiving *The Jeshua Letters* all the more remarkable, for the being from which they were received identifies himself clearly as the historical Jesus.

The message contained in these letters is radical, and possibly threatening, depending on your perspective. What I am most certain of is that my childhood prayers have been answered. In fact, it is clear that the whole of my life has been a servant of that Answer, patiently showing me all the places – both inside and out – where Christ is not, as well as gently preparing me to hear the Master, helping me to understand that feeling of the five-year-old boy.

My own journey of awakening is not so very different from your own. In fact, I have come to see that it is your own, as yours is mine. For our participation in this grand mystery we call 'life' is one of a very sacred intimacy. Though on the surface our lives can appear to be quite different, at very deep levels it becomes virtually impossible to distinguish one from the other.

It is, then, the open, wholehearted sharing of our seemingly separate journeys that helps us all move closer to the Answer we are seeking, regardless of how we ask the Question.

If, by my sharing *The Jeshua Letters*, even one reader gains light on his or her path or is compelled to ask fundamental questions in a new way, then the time I have spent writing this book will have been more than worthwhile.

Now, many years later, my wish for you remains the same: may your own journey be blessed with the same Light with which He, for all these years now, has blessed mine.

Though we may never meet face-to-face, I want you to know I am grateful for each time you choose forgiveness or are willing to look within and question the ego's 'little mind,' for every time you are willing to open to new revelations, are moved to new creations, or choose to extend Love to one and all.

I and many others walk with you – you are not alone. For what Jeshua says is true, "This we do together, until all of Creation is returned to being only the praise of God's Presence.

Blessings to you!

Jayem
July, 2021

Chapter One

*Each and every one of you
is here for but one reason:
to realize the Truth
and to come Home again.*

July 20, 1987

"Are you okay?" asks Kendra.

"Huh?" For a moment I turn my head and look at her, then just as quickly look away again. "Yeah, I'm fine," I mutter halfheartedly, as I sink back into the couch, resting my feet on the wicker chest that serves as a coffee table.

Leaning forward from her position next to me, Kendra picks up her cup of tea, takes an unhurried sip, then pauses with the cup held between her hands. "Are you sure you are okay?"

I don't want to talk about it. Yes, I do. No, I don't. I have been distracted all day. Begrudgingly, I realize that watching television is not going to drown it out after all. Technology has failed me again.

"I had a, uh, rather interesting experience during meditation this morning. I guess it *is* preoccupying me a bit."

"A bit? That's an understatement! You haven't really been here since your body walked through the door over an hour ago!" She puts her cup down and leans back, slightly turned now so that she can look directly at me. She is not going to let me out of this one.

I sigh, let my shoulders relax, and fall into the memory of what happened this morning...

Let's see. The iron is plugged in, so while it heats up I'll just buzz into the kitchen and make my morning smoothie. A little juice, a little yogurt, two eggs, a dash of vanilla, one large banana, and two tablespoons of spirulina. I hit the button on the blender, and in an instant the whole thing is dark green.

"Ah, one of life's beautiful pleasures," I think to myself. A few gulps

1

later, the pleasure has disappeared.

Checking the iron, I frown. It is still not quite ready. Well, I can make sure everything is in my briefcase. Papers? Check. Glasses? Check. Pen? Check. Certs? Where are the Certs? Why am I always out of Certs? Is there a Certs monster living in my briefcase?

I shrug my shoulders as I close my briefcase, setting it down in the foyer. I just won't get too close to anyone when I'm speaking today.

At last the iron is ready, and in a few minutes I am donning an almost perfectly ironed shirt. Buttons are fastened and tails tucked in as I head for the bedroom to grab a tie, when it happens.

Out of nowhere, and for no apparent reason, I am hit with the sudden impulse to sit in meditation. The force of the thought is so powerful that it quite literally stops me in my tracks.

Finally managing to recover, my only reaction is: "This is absurd. I am not scurrying about like this because I have time to kill." Nevertheless, the thought persists (if you can call a feeling that resounds throughout your body and is also a voice seemingly coming from all around you, a 'thought').

In fact, the experience is so impactful that my priorities suddenly switch as I walk back out to the living room, and plop down on the couch. Crossing my legs, I glance for a moment out the window at the waters of Puget Sound, where a tanker slowly makes its way past Vashon Island.

"Really, this is absurd." The voice of reason is softer now, making one last attempt to win my attention.

I begin to breathe softly, gently, rhythmically. In time my eyes naturally close, and I am increasingly aware of the myriad of thoughts whirling arid swirling and tumbling through my mind. At first they seem to gobble me up, eliciting momentary emotions, generating yet other thoughts in reaction. Slowly I become more and more the witness of this display of mindstuff, releasing attachment to content, resting more and more into awareness itself.

There comes now a growing sense of peace, of ease, as when churning waves begin to melt back into a vast and quiet sea. The thoughts grow fewer and fewer, until there is only silence. My breath is barely perceptible, sea of mind calm, clear, empty. That the meditation experience has been reduced to physiological mechanisms of the "relaxation response" by the God of Science means little when compared to the feeling of this most marvelous experience. It is the most natural of the most natural.

Perfect stillness begins to give way, but not to the usual rebirth of thoughts. Out of emptiness there emerges a soft, golden light, like a pinprick star in the dark of night. It grows effortlessly, steadily, expanding and expanding, coming closer and closer until it completely fills the field of my inner vision, until it suffuses my entire being, until there is nothing but that supernal light.

Kendra has been listening with rapt attention as I describe the experience.

"That's it, Kendra. I know this probably sounds corny, but that is it."

She has a puzzled look on her face, so needs to say nothing.

"I mean, that place, that *feeling*. If I could *live* in that feeling, that place, there would be nowhere else to go, nothing to strive for, nothing and nowhere to be or become. Am I making sense?"

Why is she smiling? Why are her eyes glowing?

"Oh, Marc! That is wonderful!" Kendra softens a bit, then continues. "You are very fortunate, you know."

Her statement stops me. I stare at her for a long while.

"Fortunate? Kendra..."

"Marc," she interrupts, "do you know how many people would love to experience that state? You are the one who has a library full of books from every culture, every philosophical perspective, every religion. You know that, at their heart, they **all** talk in varying terms of this type of experience."

She has obviously missed the point. Probably because I hedged a bit when I recounted the story. I notice my breath coming a little faster now, and feel a growing tension in my jaw.

Kendra is silent, but her eyes are riveted on me, silently questioning my lack of enthusiasm. No longer able to hold it within myself, I break the silence. "It's that, uh, well, there was a little more to it than that."

"More to it? What was more to it? Marc," she asks imploringly, "what is more to it?"

"Kendra," I pause and turn to look at her, "do you promise not to, well, say anything?"

"You aren't ever going to be able to say anything again if you don't fess up!" she cries as she lovingly, but not so gently, pokes me in the ribs.

I look away, not at anything in particular, but rather back into a memory still fresh and alive, the kind of memory that I somehow know will **always** remain that clear.

"I opened my eyes, and the pinprick of light was right in the center of the room. Out of the heart of that light there began to emerge a form, an image of someone. It appeared as if it were dressed in long, radiant robes of some kind. The form began gliding toward me, becoming more and more distinct, and yet was surely identical with the Light from which it sprang."

Growing more comfortable with the sharing of this experience, I turn to look at Kendra. "As the form came closer, I suddenly recognized him. It was as if a friend not seen for many years has just walked around the corner, and in the instant you lay your eyes on him you **know** who it is without asking, without any deliberation. But in this case there was also the recognition that I had not seen him with my physical eyes. Does that make sense?"

Kendra's face reveals her answer: one of agreement, of acceptance—one that allows me to continue.

4

"He came closer and closer, and I felt an increasing intensity of energy, like waves of joy and warmth, until his eyes were all I could see. And then his eyes seemed to pour right through me, and I felt like I was dissolving into them, into those incredibly peaceful eyes."

Pausing now, I am not certain whether to continue, but Kendra is not about to let me stop. Her expression is one of curiosity. She studies me for a moment.

Damn. Now I am cornered. I have seen that look before. She is not going to let me go anywhere until I confess all.

"What else?"

"He communicated with me, or to me, I guess."

"And?" She won't even let me catch my breath now. "What did he say?"

My shoulders begin to hunch a bit, chin dropping to my chest. "He said that he has a message to deliver to me. He said it was about the work he is doing, or something like that."

"And?"

She can be so unrelenting!

Why am I struggling with this? Kendra has been with me through it all. Every high, every low. Even the very lowest of lows. She knows me better than anyone—maybe even better than I know myself—and she still loves me! If that is not a miracle, then there are no miracles.

The hell with it. The FBI she is not. I blurt out the rest. "He said I had known him during his lifetime, and he, uh, he told me his name."

I continue softly. "It is a name, a lifetime, which has been an enigma, it seems, for the whole world."

"Well? If you are attempting to try my patience, you are succeeding!"

"Okay, okay! He said I am familiar with him as 'Jeshua.'"

5

"You mean *the-e-e-e* Jeshua? The one we all know as Jesus?"

"Yeah, *that* Jeshua."

Now Kendra is quite animated. "Well, what else did he say? What is his message? Oh, Marc, this is more marvelous than I thought, than I *can* think! What is he going to, when is he...?"

"Hold on!" I throw up my hands, demanding silence.

"What is so marvelous about it all? Kendra, out of the heart of a nice, peaceful meditation, this being has emerged, announced casually that his name is Jeshua, that he was, and is, known as Jesus, that he is going to give me some message, and to, well, to top it off, he said that I knew him!"

"So, what's the big deal?"

"What's the big deal? God, do you think I want this to happen? Look, I will admit that I am open to reading about this kind of thing, but, it's just that, well. . ."

She places her hand on my arm. "It is just that *what*, Marc?"

"It is just that this *scares* me. I mean, it's all well and good to examine metaphysics and the like from the standpoint of an observer. That is what the intellect gives us: room between us and the experience itself! Nothing has to change, you see? I can read books, go to workshops and lectures, do all that sort of thing, but part of me can still be safe! Besides, what if it is all one big ego trip? What if I am making it all up?"

Her smile fades as she realizes my fear is real. She sits reflectively for a moment, takes a cigarette out of the pack sitting next to her cup of tea, picks up her lighter, then relaxes back into the sofa.

Still looking down, she asks: "Do you remember what I shared with you about my session with Jeremiah?"

Her question seems to trigger the memory, and it all rushes forward into my consciousness, as if someone had slipped by the security guards to my archives, picked a file off an obscure shelf in a dimly lit corner, and blown the dust off, revealing the label:

> *Jeremiah. Non-physical entity channeled by Billie Ogden. Kendra is given bizarre, unverifiable information March 1987. File for future reference.*

"Yeah, I remember. We met for lunch at that cafe in Ballard."

"Do you remember what I shared with you?"

"Sort of."

She knows I just don't want to open the file on this. Recognizing my reluctance, she sits up a little straighter and speaks more firmly. "Jeremiah, if you will remember, gave me some rather startling information about you, me, and about Jesus. Don't you recall how excited I was about it?"

"Okay, okay. I remember, but I'd conveniently forgotten it, until now."

"Don't you think it's interesting that a channeled entity you have never even seen would say that you and I had known each other then, and that we had been present when Jesus gave his Sermon on the Mount? And I hadn't even mentioned your name!"

I wince. Now it is my turn to pick up a cigarette. I turn it over and over in my hand, watching little strands of tobacco spill out. I don't even smoke.

Kendra continues. "I told you then, and I'll tell you again. When Jeremiah said that, it was like somebody throwing the shutters open. Marc, there just isn't any doubt in my mind about it, even if you insist that it is too far-fetched. And now you are essentially being told something similar. Why are you having such a hard time with this?"

Tired of picking off strands of tobacco from between my fingers, I toss the cigarette down.

"You could always go see Jeremiah, and ask him what is going on."

I sigh, get up off the sofa, and stroll over to the glass doors, opening them a bit wider in order to feel the breeze which is beginning to kick up. It is probably a scout from the rain gods always hiding in the Northwest.

The thought of dealing with yet another one of those invisible souls—or entities, or discarnate beings, or whatever they are—is just not very attractive to me.

I begin speaking without turning to face her. "You know, nearly three years ago I was riding in the back of a friend's car, on the way home from Seattle where we had been attending a business seminar. In the midst of our conversation, Lyndia turned to me and suggested that I go see Jonah, that she had just been hit with the feeling that it would be good for me to do. Heck, I thought she was talking about a band or something. She hesitated, then explained that Jonah was a channeled entity."

Turning back to Kendra now, I continue. "God, the hair stood up on my arms! But then I realized it wasn't because of fear; it was because her suggestion was, well, right. I had never even remotely considered such a thing; it smacked of fairytale 'woo woo' stuff. But I went. And somehow nothing has ever been quite the same. It was as if Jonah knew why I had come, and he left no doubt that he knew me through and through."

Returning to the couch, I plop myself down. Kendra still has not lit her cigarette, which is just fine with me.

"He said some things that sent wave-like sensations through me, sensations that were some sort of recognition of the truth of what he shared. Some of what he said keeps rising to the surface of my mind from time to time, and I remember knowing somehow that it was particularly important, though I had no idea why it felt that way. He said:

> *My friend, ye have been what would be termed*
> *as a philosopher many times.*

Is it not so again?
Indeed, ye were—
in that which ye would understand
as "past incarnation"—
associated with that of a Great One,
a great master.
Be of assuredness ye were not this Great One,
but ye were in association with this one."

I look at Kendra and quickly anticipate her question. "No, it never occurred to me to ask who this 'Great One' was. As he spoke I was getting pins and needles up and down my spine. I couldn't think, let alone talk. In fact, Jonah said it would be good to pause, as I had much to ponder.

"Since then, I have had a rash of what might be called 'mystical' experiences, not to mention odd coincidences, hunches, and feeling drawn to people and books—as if some invisible magnet was pulling me first one direction, then another. And then, one innocent Saturday morning, I heard Jonah speaking to me. I jumped out of bed and scribbled down the words, complete with his trademark phrases like 'for goodness sakes' and 'ye' instead of 'you.' Do you have any idea how wary I was of that?"

"Of course I do! And don't forget the time at the lecture in Bellevue, when you heard him tell you he would speak directly to you—hours before the evening actually started and then he got up and walked right to you, basically announcing to everyone that he had been communicating with you."

It is not a memory one can forget, but she knows that.

"Yes! And I was, I *am*, still wary!"

She finally lights her cigarette, and takes a long, reflective draw of it. "You know, Marc, if you are suspicious of Jeremiah, you could always ask Jonah.

My reply takes no forethought. "Kendra, I just don't want to run off and ask some being who somehow inhabits a human body from

9

time to time what I am experiencing right now. But I will leave my options open, okay? I prefer to work on this myself."

She is watching, studying me. I can feel it. What subtle information is she picking up?

"For over three years now you have cultivated a deep admiration for the love and guidance Jonah gives, and you also know from experience that his counsel is impeccable. What could he possibly say that frightens you so?"

That's it. That is what she was picking up. Fear.

I turn a bit toward her, bending my leg and placing my foot under the other thigh. It doesn't feel right, so I try the other way. It's no good either. Finally I put my feet back on the floor. "Look, it seems to me that there are only two options here. Jonah could either reply that it is happening, or he could reply that it is not happening—that it is all my grandiose imagination."

Kendra looks baffled. "So what's wrong with that?"

"Kendra, don't you see? If it *is* happening, then I will have to do something with it! And if I am somehow making it all up, I really will have a problem to deal with, the kind that usually requires the help of a shrink, who will probably have to visit me on his rounds at Western State Hospital!"

"Is that what you are afraid of?"

"I think I am afraid of **both** outcomes. Right now, I would just as soon avoid the whole issue."

"Look, aren't you ultimately in control here? Why not go with this for awhile, and if it doesn't seem right you can always chuck it. You do not have to share any of it with anyone if you don't want to."

She is right of course. The obvious truth seems to calm me a bit. I'm breathing easier now.

"Well, Jeshua did say that I should begin writing down whatever is communicated. That if, when he is present, I would simply focus my awareness on him as I open my eyes, I will be able to maintain the connection. I don't suppose that could possibly hurt anything, could it?"

Turning my head toward the window, I notice that the warm summer sun has disappeared behind a small bank of deep blue clouds hovering over the top of Vashon Island. The rain gods have revealed themselves.

Without turning back, I continue speaking. "There is one other thing. I realized this morning that it is not the first time I have had this contact."

Kendra sits up quickly, resting her hand on my arm. "It isn't? When…?"

"A few weeks ago, when we were all camping at the beach."

⌒∞⌒

It is early morning, the dawn beginning to melt away the night. I walk along a sandy shore at water's edge, gazing first to the right, out to a cloudless horizon; then ahead to distant, steep cliffs, where a barely perceptible waterfall pours silently down to meet the sea, crashing majestically into giant boulders at the base of the cliffs.

An eagle suddenly leaves its perch high atop the towering evergreens that blanket the sloping hillsides to the left. Its giant wings move powerfully through the air; piercing eyes survey all that lies below. There is no question whose country this is.

It has become a habit. Since we first stumbled upon this glorious place, we have come here at least once a year. Building camps out of the plentiful driftwood, exploring the endless pools created by the outgoing tides, and standing awestruck beneath a canopy of stars that simply cannot be seen anywhere remotely near civilization. Luckily it is not one of those beaches found easily, unless one already knows the way.

I walk from our camp to the northernmost end of the beach, eyes dancing momentarily with the eagle soaring across an empty sky. I come to my favorite "just sitting" rock, large enough to keep me just above the surf. Squatting on my haunches and watching the surf pound against the rock, I begin to sense an incredible grace and beauty: the rock and the surf are playing together. Staring down at this exquisite interplay, the rhythm penetrates me until I feel what I hear.

There is an odd feeling beginning to grow within me. Not quite like an ache, and certainly not painful. It is more like a faint hum, a vibration. I feel it in the center of my body, near my heart. Moving now, it expands as it rises to fill my head. It seems so odd to be both feeling and passively witnessing this strange little phenomenon.

Hello, Marc.

The words emerge out of that vibration, as clear and distinct as if someone were talking into my ear. With them, the vibration seems to have changed somehow, and I begin to feel an energy, a warmth, unlike any sensation I have ever felt. It is sublime, and peaceful beyond description.

The words startle me, for there is an unmistakable sense of familiarity, as when the person you love most in the whole world calls and, when you answer the phone, they simply say "hello" and you know who it is.

> *I am glad that you have come to this point*
> *of being willing to allow*
> *this communication to take place.*
> *Rest assured that I will be speaking with you more*
> *often in the future.*

I cannot maintain the connection. The energy fades, and I again hear the surf pounding in its dance against the boulder just below me. I see the sunlight flicker across the ocean, and I feel the breeze—now blowing strongly—against my skin. I realize that I have not been aware of any of these things: not surf, nor breeze, nor sunlight.

Shaking my head, I rise, but painfully. My legs are stiff. How long have I been sitting like this?

What was that?" I mutter to myself as, finally, I am able to move my legs. Climbing carefully off the boulder, I jump the last few feet down into the sand warmed by a sun which has now risen quite high into the morning sky.

I begin walking back to camp, and suddenly there is trepidation. I resist. "No, it cannot be." I know this being, somewhere within myself, yet I cannot name him. Or perhaps I refuse to.

Back at camp, friends are stirring, breakfast begun. I sit quietly, watching gentle waves roll into shore and recede back into the sea, comforted by that timeless, rhythmic sound, while emotions stir somewhere deep inside me as if from a place unknown. Or is it a place merely forgotten?

"Do you want some more tea?" I ask, after recounting my experience at the beach.

⌒⌒

Kendra doesn't answer. She sits motionless, looking not so much at me as through me.

I walk into the kitchen and put the kettle on to boil. "Peppermint again?"

She gets up from the sofa, walks to the kitchen entrance, and leans against the wall. I don't think she heard me ask what kind of tea she wants, so peppermint will have to do.

"I remember now." Her voice is soft, eyes staring off into memories. "I remember glancing over and seeing you sitting on that log, aimlessly kicking your feet through the sand, just staring out at the ocean. It struck me that something was going on with you, but it didn't seem appropriate to disturb you, so I continued helping with breakfast."

I put the teabag in the ceramic pot and pour boiling water into it. Replacing the lid, I turn back to the stove, this time remembering to turn the heat off.

"Marc, I think you need to accept that something is going on here, don't you?"

I take the lid off the teapot, bend over and peer into the now slightly colored water, steam rising to warm my cheeks. Yep, it is starting to smell like peppermint.

Replacing the lid, I turn to face her. "Yeah, something is happening here. But it perplexes me, to say the least. I didn't ask for it, and I don't know what to do with it, or even why it is happening. I guess it is a little disorienting."

"That is a brilliant observation!"

The sparkle in her eyes, together with a loving jab into my ribs, helps release a growing pressure with me.

"You know, Kendra, the whole bent of my own spiritual path has been to the East."

My own statement triggers a stream of memories, still images sweeping by, comprising the motion picture of my spiritual and philosophical pursuits: initiation into the art of meditation nearly twenty years ago, college days spent drinking in the sublime beauty of the **Tao Te Ching**, the succinctness of Zen Buddhism, the rich and timeless mystical poetry of the **Upanishads**, the fascinating story of the warrior Arjuna in the **Bhagavad Gita**. Later, the transformative but sublime practice of yoga; hours, weeks, months, years of postures; breathing; deepening awareness; letting go in body, mind, and spirit; endless mantras dissolving into the clear and empty space of samadhi. There were experiences of the Siddhis, or 'powers': telepathy, astral travel, out-of-body, past-life recognitions. Warned that these things are but passing phenomena, I had let them go. All these images and more, swiftly seen in but an instant.

Our eyes meet, two friends so close that we do not so much share our lives with one another as blend together. The boundaries of our separate lives are grey, overlapping, flowing into and out of one another. She already knows all these things.

"You know, if a god from the Hindu pantheon had appeared—like

Krishna, or maybe Rama, or maybe a good ol' Zen Patriarch, heck, the Buddha himself!—then I don't think I would have any trouble with this. It would fit, wouldn't it? But Jesus? *Jeeeeezzzus*, Kendra!"

We stand and continue looking deep into each other's eyes, recognizing the unintended pun.

Finally, I break the silence. "You want that tea now?"

Kendra takes the cup, cradling it in both hands, savoring the warmth it brings. Without looking up, she asks quietly: "Just what is a philosopher, anyway?"

"It comes from Greek, two words, actually: 'philo,' which basically means love, and 'sophia,' which means wisdom. Philo sophia: the love of wisdom. A philosopher is a lover of wisdom."

∽

It is later in the day now, and I am alone. Sitting down on the couch and crossing my legs, I relax, gazing into the last traces of a soft and nurturing sunset.

My gaze becomes progressively less focused, my breathing calmer, more rhythmic. It feels as if my eyes are withdrawing into my head and—as has happened before—they begin to naturally draw upward. There is a sensation, as if my consciousness is becoming focused in the front of my brain, just at the back of my forehead. My surroundings begin to recede from awareness, allowing recognition of an inner environment to emerge.

Now there is a sense of movement, and I am led by someone toward what appears to be a door. It opens, and I glide forward through a tunnel of magnificent, pulsating lights. As I near the end there is a bright light, which begins to take on the form of a man in radiant garments. The face is now familiar.

> *Now, we begin.*
> *Begin to open your eyes, Marc.*
> *Yet allow your awareness to rest with Me.*

The words are both heard and seen, appearing against an empty backdrop. But more than this, I can *feel* them.

> *I am the one*
> *the world knows*
> *as Jesus,*
> *and now you have come*
> *to where I AM.*
>
> *Our first meetings*
> *will be brief.*
> *It should be viewed as*
> *an exercise for you*
> *in learning to acclimate*
> *to what may be called My frequency.*
>
> *In truth,*
> *where I AM is never*
> *inaccessible to you,*
> *nor to any of the Father's sons,*
> *for that is,*
> *of course*
> *who you are;*
> *each and everyone of you.*
>
> *And the time of remembrance*
> *is upon you.*
> *Who among you will choose to awaken*
> *from the dream you chose to dream*
> *so very long ago?*
> *What I will share with you*
> *during these first communications*
> *is not what you would call*
> *"profound wisdom."*
>
> *However,*
> *if you dwell upon what I will share with you,*
> *it can, indeed,*
> *accelerate your own journey home.*

I have been with you always.
Always,
you have known Me.
You are a servant of the Light
many call God.

It is all you have ever been,
even throughout the many experiences—
what you call "incarnations"—
you created in order to hide
from the truth you have always been.

It is permissible
to relinquish your dream.
It can serve you no longer.
It has brought you to the recognition—
through your experience—
of all the forms of avoidance
the human soul has ever devised,
all because it deems itself
unworthy of its heritage!
I will share with you
My final message
to the sons of the Living God.
When this task is completed,
I shall return to where I AM, awaiting the heralding
of the New Age of Light
upon this physical plane.
It is soon to be manifest.

Now,
I will leave you.
I would endeavor to impress upon you
the conviction of the Truth you know.
Trust your inner voice.
It neither fails
nor deceives you.

It is in silent humility

that the voice of the Father speaks.
Do know that I,
the one you know as Jeshua,
am indeed with you always,
throughout eternity.

Rest in peace.

Amen.

As his energy fades away I gradually come back to my everyday reality. Come back? Where did I go? What went where? What does it mean to "come to where I AM"? Where is that? What have I left without moving a muscle? My "dream"? With a sudden start, I look around me; stereo, fireplace, plants on the balcony moving in the wind.

I recall how Bishop Berkeley, an eighteenth-century philosopher, had once argued that our experience is very much a dream. Having heard enough of it, a student walked outside, shouting that he would refute the good Bishop's outlandish philosophy, and promptly kicked a stone with all his might, breaking his toe! Of course, he had missed the point, but part of me wants very much to kick the stone, too.

I begin to have a sneaking suspicion that I will not find an understanding for this experience by looking around me. And that is disconcerting.

⌘

August 15, 1987

Now, we begin.

Such Love have I
for the sons of God,
be they momentarily identified
as male or female for—
in Truth—
the Son is One.

The Son is that

which springs forth eternally
from the Holy Father
which is unspeakable,
and yet is ever present fullness.

Therefore,
the Love I feel
is the Love I AM.
This term signifies
not merely I as "Jeshua,"
but the Truth and Reality
of what we all are.

Allow yourselves to feel
the truth of this,
that each and everyone of you
is here but for one reason:
to realize the Truth
and to come home again.

Never upon the earth
has the opportunity to do so
been such as it is now.
Yet even when the son
stands at the door and knocks,
and the Father has opened the door,
there remains a choice to be made.
What will be your choice?

Amen.

Kendra places the communication down on the table, but does not yet take her eyes from it. "Sorry it took me so long to read. Your chicken scratch is horrible!"

"It seems to come so fast that I can barely keep up with it. Even I have a hard time reading my own writing. Maybe I should learn shorthand!"

Now she smiles, and lifts her eyes from the paper resting between us.

"I want you to know that it feels good to me, Marc. I encourage you to go ahead with this thing, whatever it is to be."

I fidget a little. God, it would be nice to have her say it all sounded trite and worthless.

"'The Son is One.' When he said that, it struck me quite deeply, but, hell, I don't know." I get out of my chair and walk over to check on the ming tree. I *never* check the plants. Even though I profess to love houseplants, it's possible they could be dead for months before I would notice.

"Marc, may I make a suggestion?"

"Of course. Suggest away!"

"When you go on vacation to Molokai in a few weeks, why not spend some time contemplating all this? Maybe you'll get some answers on why it's happening and on what is happening. It seems important to me, somehow. What do you think?"

I do not need to think about that suggestion. "No way! The last thing I want to do is try to figure this out. I am going to kick back, unwind, and just be a normal tourist. My main task is to soak up as much of that glorious Hawaiian sun as possible, and *all* my energy is going into that!"

I guess the plant will live, even with my negligence. Returning to the table, I plop down in the chair and pick up the communication.

"Look, I feel that I do need to go with this experience. Yet something in me doesn't really want to. But I know that I can always burn the stuff, or at least tuck it away in a box and bury it somewhere."

"So what are you going to do?"

"For now, not much. If and when it happens, it happens. What I *will* do is make sure I'm never too far from a writing tablet, and, heck, if any more communications come, maybe I'll jot down a few notes. You know: where I am, what is going on, that sort of thing."

A smile breaks across my face, and I look at Kendra. She returns my smile, with a question. "What are you thinking?"

"Oh, I just got this image of my grandchildren opening an old trunk filled with their grandpa's artifacts, including these old and yellowed pages of weird notes and conversations with an invisible friend. When they ask their mom about it, she'll reply, 'Well, that's why they had to lock your grandpa up, dear! Now you just put that away and go play out in the yard.'"

Kendra is laughing now, shaking her head. "You have such a weird sense of humor!"

A few moments pass, and now she looks at me, a bit more thoughtfully. "Marc, how did you feel about Jesus while you were growing up?"

The sudden shift in our conversation catches me off guard, and seems to unlock a chestful of memories. I see myself going to church on Sundays with my parents. Endless rounds of sermons and Sunday school lessons. **That** part I didn't like very much.

"My father would drop me off in front of the church for Sunday school, and I would pretend to be heading inside, but as soon as he was around the corner, off I would be! I would go downtown and spend my offering on a chocolate shake."

Kendra's eyes are wide with surprise, but they are smiling. "You! That's, that's almost sacrilegious!"

I smile at the memory. "Well, hang me at dawn. But I remember feeling very good about Jesus, when I could manage to separate him from all the dogma. I felt like here was this being who **knew** something. I mean, **really** knew something. I felt like he was somebody you could really trust."

Her voice becomes a little softer now. "Why can't you trust him now?"

"Kendra! That was a Jesus coming to me through someone else's filter! He lived in stories, and told parables that were like Rorschach ink blots. And he lived safely in history! That Jesus is easy to trust! You can believe anything about him you want to, and how is he going to defend himself?"

Without moving her head, she lifts her eyes and looks directly at me. "Maybe by making house calls."

She has stopped me dead in my tracks.

"Are you saying that you believe this Jeshua is that Jesus?"

"Isn't that what he said?"

"Yes, but..."

"How did it *feel* when he said it?"

She rests her chin in her hand now, and looks right at me.

Turning my head to look out the window, I answer her softly. "As good and as real as those chocolate shakes used to taste."

But I can't let it go at that. Emotion begins to build within me; a struggle to remain convinced that Jeshua is not Jesus. No matter what it *feels* like to me, this experience just cannot be real. Well, not **that** real.

"Look, Jesus lives in the pages of the Bible, and in obscure esoteric texts, and in the hopes of some people's hearts, but I cannot believe that he appears out of some field of light during the course of a meditation in twentieth-century America!"

I drop my head a bit. "Besides, even if he does, this is not the message empires have been built on, that millions of people have pinned the hopes of their soul on. God, Kendra, I can't share a message like this, from such a source as him! They'd, they'd..."

"Crucify you?" She completes my thought, with more than a slightly bemused look on her face.

"Yes!" I blurt out my reply, then quickly catch myself. "Well, probably not literally, but I just don't want the hassle."

We both grow quiet. "Marc."

"Yeah?"

"What if 'they' have been wrong?"

Chapter Two

*Never have the
thoughts of the world
been yours.
They are illusion.
Therefore,
so is your unhappiness.*

Fagan's Beach, Molokai
August 30, 1987

Awakening suddenly, I realize it is quite early. There isn't a trace of daylight. I am half dressed before recognizing a feeling, a sense of urgency that compels me to be up, dressed, and out the door. Surely urgency is laughable here on this most quiet—and Hawaiian—of islands, where it seems that nothing has ever been urgent at all.

I drive along the narrow, quiet road as it curves and winds its way along the coastline, passing tropical farms which grow farther and farther apart, until there are no more. My mind starts racing: "Why am I out here? Just where do I think I am going?" It is a road that I have traveled only once before—in daylight—when I visited Halawa Valley, where the oldest archaeological remains of Hawaii's ancient inhabitants lie obscured, reclaimed by dense and lush tropical jungle. It is a road which becomes narrower and narrower, with hairpin twists and turns. And here there are no streetlights to guide me.

A subtle change in light occurs as day begins to hint at its arrival. Suddenly, I slam on the brakes and come to a stop. Quickly backing up, I can now see a small, overgrown farm road. It appears to slope down some fifty feet to a gate. With a continuing sense of urgency, I am out of the car and over the fence in the blink of an eye.

Plunging into the dense grasses towering three feet over my head, I veer to my left for no reason other than it feels right. Finally, I break through into low, sparse foliage, quickening my pace, the urgency compelling me from within.

There is just enough light to turn the world around me into faint shadows. I am running now, until I come to a knoll of large, volcanic boulders. Scurrying to the top, I hear the surf somewhere below me. My heart is racing. I am excited, though I haven't any idea where I am, or why.

It occurs to me to sit in meditation, enveloped by soft breezes whose

24

touch easily quiets my body, mind, and breath, until there is only crystalline awareness, sublime well-being.

I now feel a subtle, growing warmth as the rising sun begins to caress my body. Slowly opening my eyes, I explode in joyous laughter. It is so beautiful here! The boulder which supports me is at the top of a knoll just to one end of a small, horseshoe-like cove, and I face out across the channel to Maui, watching now as the sun rises like a fiery god into a lightly clouded sky. It is the most natural of responses to simply give thanks. Though my eyes are open, that now familiar feeling begins. I see that golden Light, then hear a familiar Voice.

Now, we begin.

It is in seeking for,
and asking of,
That which is the highest,
within you and without you,
that one comes, therefore, to the highest.

Beloved Son,
you who would journey so long
without Me,
know that you indeed have come home again.

I am That I AM.
Never have you been without Me,
for your worlds are but
a moment of illusion.

I would speak with you
at this most glorious time
of That which alone is Real.

I would speak with you
of That which alone is Life.
I would speak with you
of That which alone can enable the voyager
of a thousand worlds to come home again.

Beloved Son,
what is Real, I AM.
What is unreal exists not.
I am the Light and the Life of all.
My radiance knows no boundary,
My purity is not tainted.

In that beginningless beginning,
I brought you forth as the thought
of perfect Love in form.
That alone is what you are.

The earth is My body.
Embrace it,
for it will teach you of Me.
The world is your illusion.
It can teach you nothing,
for what is not Real contains
no knowledge of Me.

Beloved Son,
your soul is My breath.
When first I created you,
already were you complete.
Never have you deviated from
That which I created you to be.
You are My delight,
and in you know I that which I AM.

Your only thought has been one;
Separation from Me.
Upon this rests the creation
of millennia of illusions.
The worlds you have experienced,
the fears, the doubts,
the striving, the achievements,
all you have ever imagined
you ever have been or done,
and all you can ever imagine

you ever could be and do,
is but a moment's imagination.
All rests on that one thought.

This I give you as
the Way of Life:
releasing this thought
brings forth into recognition
what alone is Real.

No striving brings
the Son to the Father.

No prayer and supplication
can achieve it,
for these things reside in the world of
your creations,
and thus have nothing
of Reality in them.

Your journey is not.
Always you rest in Me,
always you abide in Me.
What alone is Real
resides within you
as your very soul.
It is your heart,
and can be truly known.
Silence is the threshold of this wisdom divine.

Often I will come to you,
often I shall speak to you,
for you have wearied of your journey.
Now, you are home with Me.

I repeat,
for those who will choose to hear
what is now given forth:
the Way is easy,
and without effort.

For that which comes of effort
is of your world,
and not of Me.

I am known only
when you choose to surrender
in fullness
the one thought you have ever entertained,
for upon it
rests the arising of all worlds.
I alone am the end of the world.
Herein lies the peace
that passes all understanding.

Amen.

The light fades. I sit in stillness for a long, long time. My world has completely stopped.

I rise slowly and walk down to the beach, feeling the warm sand beneath my feet, watching the sunlight dance like sparkling diamonds across the surface of gentle waves. Undressing, I walk into the surf, soothed and held by tropical waters. And now the tears begin. There is no resistance in me. Tears flow freely as I stand waist deep in the ocean.

I am speechless, thoughtless. There seems to be only the feeling of the waves lapping against my stomach, and a waterfall of my tears running down over my cheeks, onto my chest.

Coming out of the water, I feel as if all my energy is gone. Collapsing in the sand, I fall into a deep sleep.

❦

"The captain has turned off the seat belt light."

The voice of an unseen stewardess jars me from a brief nap. Turning my head, I peer out the window, watching for a moment as Hawaii disappears behind me, coming to rest, no doubt, in a tiny treasure chest somewhere in my brain labeled "Fondest Memories."

Opening my carry-on, I pull out the steno pad, flip back the cover, and read the communication received at Fagan's Beach.

> **Your only thought has been one:**
> **Separation from Me.**
> **Upon this rests the creation**
> **of millennia of illusions.**

Images suddenly begin to cascade through my mind. Indians and cavalry; skyscrapers and traffic jams; hundreds of Moslems bowing toward Mecca; a priest giving confession; an Indian holy man, his body smeared in ashes; the face of a man behind bars; the chaos of the stock market; a newlywed couple whose eyes express the hope that their excitement will last forever; an old woman as she takes her last breath...

I turn my head toward the window and straighten my body to stop the onrush of images that come not one after the other, but seemingly all at once.

Can it be so simple? And just how do I release this one thought so strongly believed in—if I am to accept what Jeshua says—for "millennia"? How am I to accept that what I have believed, perhaps unconsciously, is the foundation of an illusory world that everyone else seems to believe in too?

Putting the steno pad back into its place—tucked into the bottom of my bag somewhere beneath my socks and underwear—I rest my head back into the seat, pressing the button located just inside the armrest in order to drop it back as far as possible, and deliberately turn my attention to the movie, wishing I had paid my six bucks for the headphones.

⌘

September 3, 1987

The experience on Molokai already seems far removed. I have not re-read the dictation received there since the trip home. It is stuffed into a drawer, as though a part of me is hoping the old adage is right: out of sight, out of mind.

What is this resistance, this fear, all about? Am I making up this whole experience with Jeshua? Would I even want to make it up? Memories of evenings that seem lifetimes ago float into my conscious mind—memories of having a few beers after work, playing pool, and discussing the upcoming Superbowl game—memories of a reality that feels rather attractive just now. If only I hadn't taken that philosophy class eighteen years ago—that's it! It jarred my ideas. I began to question the most obvious "facts" of life. I should have taken accounting or something, and maybe this wouldn't be happening. I would have a nice, safe job somewhere, and my evenings would not be consumed by this struggle between avoiding the experience I am having and being compelled to understand it.

Why couldn't Jeshua at least say something that makes sense? How about some winning lottery numbers? What I hear rings with the clarity of certain truth—while I hear him, but nothing of my experience in the day-to-day world seems to mesh with it. It is not just another slant on reality; it is a wholly new Reality altogether.

This inner debate spins on through my mind, without reconciliation, until the very failure of my intellect to grasp it, to pin it down in the neat boxes of logic it worships, forces me to simply shut up. Then, it begins again. That sense of warmth that grows from within, the vibrational change, and finally, the Voice:

Now, we begin.

Abide with Me yet a little while.
I wish to communicate with you now,
before you leave for your office.
Are you willing to join with Me now?

"Yes," I mutter beneath my breath. I'm sure I've already lost what little sanity I had, so why not?

Then take up pad and pen,
for I will share with you
that which is Life,
Truth,
and that which alone is Real.
I am Jeshua,
and I hear you call.
Long have I been with you,
Marc.
Since before your Lemuria
am I with you.
There is naught that will be hidden from you
in this life,
for you are coming home to the Father.

Would you not abide in peace now?
I do not speak of a moment's respite
before continuing your journey.
I speak only of the final peace
that knows no contradiction,
nor any contrast.

It is the peace
that abides in the Father,
given freely to His Son
since first was created
the thought of Separation.
I behold your thought,
and accurate it is,
no matter how incredible
you insist it seems.
For in the Father, illusion is not.
There is no separation,
for there is not the thought of it.

What I teach,
others teach.

Many are the teachers,
one is the teaching.

Your clinging to those
last threads of your separation
is the dissatisfaction you feel.
Even now,
you are keenly aware of this.
The world has lost its savor for you,
for you have transcended the world.

Abide in us, Marc.
The world in all its teachings
knows nothing of us,
the holy union of
father and son.
Few there are who would truly
relinquish their dreams.

I have spoken to you that through you
I choose to give my final message
to the Son remaining
in illusion.
And so it shall be.
The time comes quickly now,
for you are come unto the Father's presence.

Blessed are the children of Light.
Blessed,
yet unaware.
Only in the end of all journeying
is the blessing recognized.

And the blessing of the Father
resides in this:
the Son has never truly suffered,
never truly journeyed forth.
No pain has been overcome.
No effort has been expended.

When this is recognized,
there is found the end of the world,
which is always illusion,
no matter the form.

The world may be of pain,
the world may be of what many call joy,
yet beyond these is the Truth
of the Real.
It is the abode of the Father,
and this the Son has never departed.
This is the highest truth capable of expression.
This you come to now.

Despair not,
for I am with you.
Allow the dissolving
of your dreams.
What you are the Father
has created you to be,
and in this is your true joy.

This day,
allow yourself to perceive
all you experience as the ending of your illusion:
the birth of Life.
Soon I will come forth with
instructions for you.
Follow them,
for now is the time upon the earth.
Many are nearly ready
to hear the Word,
and awaken from illusion.

Go now in peace.
I love you greatly,
for Love I AM.

Amen.

It is an hour later. How am I supposed to view being stuck in this traffic jam—as "the end of my illusion"? I think to myself: "Just let it go, let the judgment of this moment go." My mind is suddenly serene, like a mountain lake without a trace of windblown ripples.

I begin to laugh as an image comes to mind. Zen Buddhist monks rise before dawn and go to the zendo, or meditation hall, to "just sit," perfecting the ability to simply be present. So what is a traffic jam, anyway? An agitation that prevents us from getting to where we think we must be? Or is it, perhaps, a zendo?

For a moment, I am a Zen Buddhist monk, but only for a fleeting moment.

∞

September 9, 1987

Now we begin.

Marc, hear Me well.
For even as you have come unto Me,
so I come now unto you.
As I have spoken,
there comes forth instruction unto you
who has asked for the end of illusion.
Follow this and,
indeed,
there will come the dawning
of what you have longed to remember.

Rest now but a moment,
and close your eyes that would show you
but the world of your illusion,
and in this rest I will come unto you,
and My presence will be as a healing unto you.
Rest now . . .

(What transpired I have never been able to put into words. It was as though all of me was melting into light. I have never felt such utter peace.)

> *And now the end of sorrow is upon us.*
> *I will go out no more from the Father's holy place.*
> *Indeed, I have overcome the world.*
> *It is not to think that the task is completed,*
> *for the only task is the salvation of the world.*
> *This we do together,*
> *until the sons of God*
> *recognize themselves as but the only begotten;*
> *Christ.*
>
> *Herein lies peace.*
>
> *Amen.*

∝∽∍

September 25, 1987

Dissatisfaction. I am feeling it again. I do not suppose that it is an experience known only by me. Is it my job? That must be it. In an instant my mind sees many aspects of my current job that could be the cause of this feeling. They range from not paying enough money to requiring too many hours. On the other hand, it **does** have its good points, such as paying the bills.

Maybe it's my current relationship. That must be it. It's great in so many ways, but...

There is something I am supposed to be doing with my life, but I do not know what it is. Maybe this is it, just what I'm doing. If it is, why doesn't it feel that way? Why do I do what I do? Why do I feel what I feel? God, sometimes I feel like Barbra Streisand singing, "What's it all about, Alfie?"

Oh, what the heck. Here I am, after all. I cannot pinpoint what the dissatisfaction is about, but it is certainly there. Get busy. Just get to work and don't think about it. Good idea. Maybe tonight I'll rent a movie, have a glass or two of wine.

Evening now. Wine poured, but not yet tasted. For some reason, I hesitate to slip the video into the VCR. I drop down on the couch and just sit.

"Damn," I think to myself. I am feeling it begin to happen again. I realize I have noticed it virtually at its inception. As that feeling grows, I leap up and scurry to find pad and pen. I may as well resign myself to receiving this communication. Maybe I am going crazy, or maybe I've already done so, in which case there can be no further harm by being ready...

Now, we begin.

First, it is for you to understand
that in virtually every instance
of your unhappiness,
there is found what we shall call
a dependence on the
illusion of circumstance.
Contemplate this for a moment,
and I believe you will easily come
to see the truth of this.

There!
That took but a moment,
did it not?
You well recognize
that in those moments just prior to
the arising of feelings you
choose to label as 'unhappiness,'
there is first the subtle thought
of circumstance.
What is circumstance, Marc?

"Well, I guess it is a place, an environment of sorts."

Yes!
A place. That is good.

Now,
come in your understanding to that
which always exists
prior to circumstance.
What will be discovered here is thought.
Your thought.
Or, better,
what you have unwittingly identified with
as being your thought.

What we are asking you to examine,
with that keen intellect
you have painstakingly developed
over the course of a multitude of lifetimes,
is simply this:
Whence the thought
which is prior to circumstances
you deem as painful?

You have noticed that we equate pain
with unhappiness in the
mental -> emotional -> physical realms.
We give the picture of arrows
to indicate that pain involves
your entire being.

If you were to well understand
how far this "being" extends,
the responsibility would paralyze you.
But all in good time.

Now,
whence thought?
Consider the distinction given you
some time ago between
that of the "world" and that of the "earth,"
It is a critical distinction.
The earth is what you would call an "entity."
Its form,

which is its quality,
is not so very different from your own.

We mean by this
that the earth freely chooses
to express in physical form,
recognizing and accepting
the inherent limitations of this choice.
It does this as all true masters do:
as a choice to delight
in the expression of that which
the Father is:
Unconditional Love that cannot
entertain fear,
or constriction of its god nature.

The earth loves you greatly,
as it does all of mankind.
It feels sadness,
and we say this directly,
not metaphorically.
This sadness is the result
of mankind's widespread refusal
of the Father's presence,
and purpose.

Separation steadfastly adhered to
by mankind
creates a disharmony in all that is,
which the earth can no longer tolerate.
Its sadness brings forth a cleansing
which now begins to express visibly.
This will accelerate
in the months and years to come.

The earth is a wise master
from whom mankind could learn
to easily provide all that is required
without the least bit of effort.

Mankind scarcely remembers
that such possibility exists.

The world is always illusion.
We see clearly the difficulty
you have with this.
Can it be true?

Must it be true?
You have already glimpsed the consequences
of recognizing this truth
in its fullness.
And that is why you resist it.

The world, Marc, means nothing.

This horrifies you,
though no longer to such a degree
that you do not already hold
within yourself
the acceptance of this truth.

Now do we give you your first key:
Your feelings emanate from your refusal
to allow this truth into
the totality of your being.

Your inner cry for the world to mean something
is the cry of everyone
who would insist on Separation
from the Father.

The total acceptance of this truth
is the death of Separation,
and signals the end of the world.

Indeed,
from the perspective upon which
mankind insists,
this does appear as horrific.

But know this:
horror at the thought of the world's end
is but the choice to believe in illusions.
We send here to you
the image of many mirrors
quietly shattering around you,
leaving naught but splendid light,
to assist in feeling how safe it truly is
to release illusion.

The world is your self-created trap.
You,
as each soul upon the earth has done,
have assisted in the creation
of this elaborate web of illusion,
and its subsequent delusions
about what is Real.

Look closely at all of your experience
as circumstance.
Is it not a perpetual struggle
to discern and grasp
what is thought to be real?

What activity does mankind
participate in,
in which he does not ascribe to it
the value of having Reality?
Mankind creates it,
then seeks it out to experience it—
again and again—
solely in order to substantiate
his belief that illusion is Reality.

Allow me to simplify.
What is illusion?
The world.
Who is its creator?

Mankind,
existing in the choice of Separation.
Mankind's quest?
To prove his creation
has the value of Reality.

Pride is the only sin
which can be said to exist.
It arose when first was held
in the thought of the Son:
"I am separate from the Father."

Incidentally,
what is being taught under the banner
of the New Age is quite true:
each incarnate soul is a co-creator,
creating the world with infinite variation.
But this is not a teaching which
fosters enlightenment,
but only the perpetuation
of illusion.
And so it continues.

The world is a web of illusion which you,
as a soul,
freely choose to be immersed within.
The web is like a vortex,
or an energy field which is the sole creation
of mankind.

Its entire foundation rests
upon Separation,
no matter what the pride
of the ego may desire
to believe.

To insist upon illusion
is to choose being bound
by this energy, or vortex.

There is no enlightenment in the world,
nor can there be.

It is this truth
that the ego of mankind
will cleverly resist
until exhaustion comes.
And of what?
A momentary thought
of Separation.
Only a fantasy.
And from this,
the arising of all worlds.
The fantasy,
in truth,
never occurred.

This is the salvation of the world:
that it does not,
nor has it ever,
existed.

This one thought is given to you
as your second key,
and can be given to anyone
seeking salvation.
Its contemplation may bring an end,
however momentary this may be,
to identification with the web of energy
which is the mind of the world.

Now,
we have come full circle,
and well you perceive the true source
of all your unhappiness.

For never have the thoughts of the world
been yours.
They are illusion.

Therefore, so is your unhappiness.
You have come to a point
where there is an acute recognition
that every moment
of unwitting identification
with the web of energy
which is the mind of the world
is the creation of pain,
no matter its interpretation
by the ego,
which would insist on its reality.

The joy of the world is a lie,
for the world is not.

Go now, Marc.
Dwell upon these things.
Know well that you hover on the brink
of shattering the mirrors
of illusion.
The veil is being rent.

What you experience,
In your own way,
is the only death which matters.
It is the death of Separation.
Well do I know what will emerge.

Remember this,
and love yourself for it.

We leave you,
yet are always with you.

Peace, I give unto you.

Amen.

October 12, 1987

"Great night to have emergency clients. Damn!" I mutter to myself while I hurry to turn off my computer, adding machine, typewriter, and radio.

It's a half-hour drive to my yoga class, which is scheduled to begin in twenty minutes. Time to fly. How can the teacher expect anyone else to be on time if he can't be there on time himself?

Grabbing my briefcase and jacket, I tear past the receptionist. "I'm out of here, Peggy!"

"Have a nice..."

Her reply goes unheard as I close the door behind me and run to the parking lot. Better play speed racer tonight.

"Great, just great!" I scream as I approach a well-known curve and see that traffic is stopped. It remains quite a distance to the light where I need to turn, and now I know I'll be late.

And then, wham! Just like that, and for no apparent reason, it happens.

No, I have not been rear-ended, though I almost wish I had. Suddenly, everything is perfectly quiet. I cannot hear the cars around me, nor even my radio. My visual field loses sight of everything, temporarily overshadowed by three words:

THE JESHUA LETTERS

My whole body is electrified, from the tip of my head to my toes. Then, just as suddenly, it is gone, and everything is back to normal.

"Where did that come from?" I wonder. I feel like I have been hit over the head. Then it strikes me. I am being asked to make this stuff public!

"Oh, no! No way!"

Finally, traffic begins to inch along. I make my way into the parking lot and, as I begin walking to the classroom, I notice that only a few of my students' cars are here. Maybe very few will be here tonight.

Now, others begin arriving, and I look at my watch. 5:55! It only took me fifteen minutes to get here? In that traffic jam? That is not possible!

∝∞⊃

On my way home from class, I impulsively turn in a different direction. "It is not too late and, besides, what are friends for?" I rationalize as I head for Kendra's house.

I rap loudly and insistently, revealing my impatience, until the door opens.

"Well, surprise of surprises! I thought maybe you had given up your body or something."

"I know, I have been a little busy of late, what with work and my yoga classes starting up again."

"So, you no longer have a phone?" She smiles, as she hangs up my coat. It is a beautiful Northwest fall evening, but the crispness in the air is beginning to whisper of changes to come. "God, that feels good!" I stand next to her wood-burning stove with the palms of my hands as close as possible without touching it.

"I know it isn't **that** cold yet, but what the heck, I love the warmth of a fire!" She settles into her new recliner, the kind that simply swallows you up and refuses to let you go, no matter what tasks are screaming at you for attention. I drop into the couch and relax, letting my eyes rest on the silent dance of the flames in the stove.

"So, how is it going?" Kendra asks.

I glance at her and realize she is interested only in the communications. "I suppose you know that is the reason I am here. Well, at least one of the reasons. I mean, I wanted to see you..."

"Don't try to apologize yourself out of that one!" She is laughing now, and I recover from a moment's embarrassment.

"I took your advice and just let myself jot this stuff down when it occurred, which hasn't been all that often, thank God. Once on Molokai, and..."

"What did he say?" she asks, sitting forward a bit.

"It, well, he, I, uh, Kendra," I mutter, "I think I would rather not get into it right now. Don't ask me why. I just feel like I would rather not. Not yet, anyway. I think I'd like some time to make sense of it myself."

Realizing my tentativeness, she asks softly, "Is it that provocative?"

I hesitate, feeling a bit self-conscious about my answer. "Well, uh, yes, it, uh, I think it is, yes."

"You **think** it is?"

Now it's my turn to sit forward on the couch. "I've read my share of metaphysical stuff over the years, and this is blowing me away."

Kendra laughs, saying, "Maybe that is the meaning of it!"

"What?"

"Maybe it's **supposed** to blow you away!"

Sighing, I tell her what happened on the way to my yoga class. "Damn, Kendra, I don't know about this! The thought of making this public makes me shudder. I'm no writer. I don't know the first thing about publishing, and besides..."

Her outburst of laughter cuts my tirade short. Feigning annoyance, though inwardly thankful for the interruption, I tilt my head slightly, turning so that I can barely see her out of the corner of my eye. "And just what is so funny now?" I ask.

"You are better entertainment than watching **The Cosby Show!**"

"Huh?"

"Marc, look. Don't forget who is ultimately in control here! You are the one in a body! You are the one who has control over the decision to publish it or not! Would you please relax about it?"

She gets up from her chair, opens the door to the stove, and throws another log inside. Sparks fly and the flames leap higher for a moment as the log drops into the embers.

Kendra turns to me, and stands there for a moment gently shaking her head. "I know I would probably be feeling different about it if it were happening to me. I'd probably totally freak out about it, like you are. But, look, may I say something?"

My turn to make a friendly jab. "So when have you ever asked permission?"

She smiles. "Marc, I just have this *feeling* about it, even if you don't want to share any more of it with me at this point. Like I said before you went on vacation, I encourage you to stay with it."

"But, Kendra, the suggestion was so clear. This doesn't seem to be meant only for me, and the thought of making it public makes me shudder!"

I put my hands on my knees and stand up quickly. "You know, I couldn't even concentrate while teaching tonight! When the class was over, I wasn't sure I was even there! I can't function with all this stuff going on! I find myself suddenly contemplating something Jeshua has said. Like tonight, all I could think about was that invisible neon billboard flashing those three words at me!"

"How did your class go?"

"What do you mean?"

"Do you think anyone noticed you were not really there?"

I thought for a moment. "A few of my students thanked me afterward, said it had been one of their favorite classes." I shake my head at the memory.

"Well, there you go! You don't really need to be there after all. And you probably thought you were important!"

"Ooooh, low blow!"

Kendra's face becomes thoughtful. "Marc?"

I feign a lack of interest. "I am not going to listen if it hits below the belt again!"

"No, no. It's just that, well, behind this resistance, there must be something impelling you to continue with it. I mean, if there wasn't, why would you bother listening to the communications at all, or think about them? I really wish you would just let it happen as it happens. Don't make any judgment about it for now, okay?"

I look at her for a long time. Boy, what would life be without those special friends that journey through it all with you sharing, supporting, encouraging, lightening the loads we somehow create for ourselves?

"Okay, okay. Well, I don't think I want to share it right now, with anyone. But can I unload on you if I need to?"

"What do you think, you nut? Now, let's have a glass of wine before you go, since it looks like the only time I am going to see you is when you think you are going crazy!"

"Well, if this continues, you may be seeing me more often than you think!"

Chapter Three

*It is always fear
of one's own death
that blocks recognition
of the Kingdom.*

November 2, 1987

Now, we begin.

Beloved brother,
for that is surely what you are,
I have come because you have asked.
I will share with you,
during the course of our encounter of this moment,
that which will reveal to you
the harmony of the Kingdom.

First,
you will notice that I favor
the use of terminology
clearly Christian,
though it should be seen that such terminology
is better viewed as Judeo-Christian.
I do this because such terms are easily identifiable
relative to the time I walked among you.
It is certainly not the only format
which could be chosen.

I am not limited,
nor are you.
The only difference of significance between us
is that I have fully acknowledged
my unlimitedness,
while you choose not to.

Marc,
over the past few years,
as you perceive the flow of your experience,
much insight has been achieved

for one good reason:
you have desired it.
Desire, then,
is the first factor required
in the process of emerging
from the sleep you have existed within
for millennia.

I am quite aware
of what you think is doubt.
Consider this:
could it be fear of the obvious?
What changes would occur in your life
were you to acknowledge
that you,
born of your desire,
had indeed brought forth
into manifest expression
the experience of joining with the mind of Jeshua,
the "Christ?"

The latter term is not a title I demanded.
It was placed upon Me
by those who refused
to fully acknowledge My message
within themselves.
The failure to do so
is always the result of fear.

Fear is the only energy
which can separate you
from the Kingdom.
It is not the "fear of God,"
but the fear of one's own self.
This is misplaced by projecting it on to God,
which must be perceived
as something wholly other.
Contemplation of this alone
can facilitate much movement

within one's consciousness.
And is not all such movement
but the surrender of limitation,
owned as self-created?

Therefore, my unlimitedness allowed Me to state,
without the least hesitation:
"I and My Father are One."

One enters the Kingdom
when the obvious truth of this statement
is acknowledged in one's own mind.
It marks the surrendering
of self-imposed limitation.
I wish it to be quite clear
that My choice of the word
"darkness" should always be equated with fear,
which is the one form of energy
you may be said to have created.

In the Kingdom,
it does not exist.
You are loved wholly.
You have never sinned.

It is the nature of the Dreamer to
believe in his Dream.
The Dream you know well.
The Reality you dimly perceive,
like the echo of a melody
faintly coming back to you.
Listen to it, and it alone.

This is where your special abilities are of value.
Sharing with others
the art of being silent
can alone assist those who seek the Kingdom
to come to a place of vulnerability,
where we can speak to them.

The Kingdom cannot be lost,
but it has been forgotten.
Yet in the forgetting is born the very substance
of genuine remembering.

We use whatever you dream
as a mechanism for your awakening.
If I may be allowed brief levity here,
though you trudge across white carpeting
with muddy feet,
we transform it into an exquisite tapestry
which will grab your attention.

Just this is the harmony of the Kingdom:
nothing, absolutely nothing,
can ever serve but to nudge the Dreamer
toward the end of his sleep.
This is why,
when I first spoke to you
several months ago,
I emphasized that
your moment-to-moment experience
is the path to your enlightenment.
It is harmonious,
and but a glimpse assures
even the most skeptical
that this is so.

You will have noticed by now
that your asking for contact with your guides
does not require our consent
for communication to occur.
Your asking is your consent
to allow what is always available to you.
It is an exercise in the release of fear.
It occurs when the Dreamer,
however dimly,
begins to perceive there is something quite odd
about the nature of the Dream.

The Dream is the entire realm of fearful experience
which has burst forth from that one initial thought:
"I am separate from God."
It occurred countless eons ago,
yet only a moment ago,
for time is but part of your Dream.

One of your guides has repeatedly emphasized
that the attitude one needs to adopt
in order to awaken from the Dream
is to "allow, allow, allow."
Asking for guidance fosters this,
and is the implicit recognition
that nothing else has worked,
that there is nothing else to be done.

Initially,
this act of allowing is horrifying
because it feels like dying,
an experience quite well known
to the separate ego!

For this reason,
the majority of seekers remain forever seekers,
searching for some form of magic that will,
in essence,
bring enlightenment to them.

This cannot work,
for awakening requires a receptiveness.
This can only occur
in the attitude of allowing,
that is,
the allowing of death to occur.

It is irrational to the separate self
that the greatest doing occurs in the act
of doing absolutely nothing.
Therefore,

"My burden is light and My yoke is easy."

No effort is required to enter the Kingdom.
Allowing is the key to the doorway
beyond the Dream of the Dreamer.
Only a moment's reflection will indicate
how tired you, Marc,
have become of your Dream.
This initially can create great conflict
as it dawns upon the Dreamer
that something is amiss,
yet his brothers perceive it not,
and all attempts to share what is felt
lead only to the frustration of failure.

One cannot make the Dream end,
because the Dreamer is part
of the Dream.
Allowing is the process
of surrendering the Dream
of the Dreamer himself.
When the Dreamer dissolves,
so, too, does his Dream.
There is then only the Kingdom,
which alone has always been.

You are an awakening Dreamer.
As I say this, you will recognize its truth:
the only difference between you
and many of our brothers
is that you recognize the dream
and the validity of allowing
as the key to the Kingdom.

An aspect of your Dream
was your journey with Me
in Canaan and Galilee.
From many sources have you been given this.
Let me confirm it for you.

You were an Essene,
and even during this present life you have encountered
many of your fellow dreamers.

You have heard that you,
together with your dear friend Kendra,
were present when I spoke to the multitudes
on the Mount of Olives.
Know that you were.
What struck you was not the essence
of the teaching delivered that day,
but the recognition that the teaching
was realized in Me.
The carpenter's son had journeyed to distant lands
and returned a master.
Such was your perception.

Thus,
the doorway to the Kingdom
became for you
as a jewel to be discovered
in the East.
You went there,
during nine consecutive incarnations,
to master the yogas and philosophies.
In this present incarnation,
you have completed your chosen course.

This ending, as you well know,
has been the recognition
that the Dreamer can master
the whole of his Dream,
yet remain enmeshed in the Dream itself.
You have discovered the very simple key—
the jewel—
and is this not the silence of allowing?

It can be said that your experience
of My sermon

was the first genuine movement
to awaken from your Dream.

Does it appear to have been a long journey?
Remember,
such a perception
is of the Dream itself.

I am going to ask that you begin spending
a little time with Me daily now.
The work I spoke of earlier
is now complete
and we can begin.

Again,
this is not a command from Me,
only a gentle reminder.
This participation is your free choice,
as always it must be.
That which I AM
knows nothing of compulsion,
for love cannot compel.
It merely attracts the seeker of Reality
to itself.

This requires no effort
but to be available,
for each and every seeker recognizes Love
because—however deeply buried—
there is the recognition
that Love is
the true being of the seeker himself.
This is never denied,
but it is repeatedly ignored.
Our task, then,
is only to gently bring the seeker
to the experience of attention
to what alone has always been:
the Kingdom.

We will end here.
I am well pleased with the ease you have come to
in attending by allowing.
Is not the journey,
no matter how fraught
with seeming dilemma and pain,
well worth it?
Bless it, all of it.

Amen

⌇

November 13, 1987

Hello, Marc.

"Hello, Jeshua."

Now, we begin.

Is it not the comfort
of absolute knowing you seek?
Is it not the comfort
of absolute union you desire?
For it is a great truth,
given earlier to you and today reinforced,
that desire is the primary key to fulfillment.
Therefore, one needs to assess the object of desire.
For this I share with you most emphatically:
what is desired is experienced,
always.
Such is the bounty of your Father's table,
such is the love of your universe:
"Ask and ye shall receive."

I would like to clarify this statement
which is, by the way, one I did make.
At a future time,
I will clarify for you precisely those teachings

found in scripture
which were given genuinely by Me;
many were not.
Through this process,
I will clarify the meaning of those teachings,
returning them to their original intention.

"Ask and ye shall receive."
It matters not what you ask for,
nor that the asking
is perhaps
what is widely known as "unconscious."
The mind has depth.
The asking of which I speak
is that which flows
from the depth of your mind.

The intent of creation,
which is the ever-present flow of the Father,
is to utilize the asking
as a mechanism for focusing that
movement of life into form.
The obstacle, of course,
is the delusory separation known
as ego.

This each of you participates in,
reflecting to yourselves
aspects of the grand illusion
which is your only creation.
As all of you are of One Mind in Truth—
the only begotten Son—
so, too,
are you of one mind as your illusion,
ego.

Never do you look upon another,
for there is no "other."
You see only yourself.

It has been spoken many times
to "Love your brother as yourself."
This is because your brother is yourself.
In loving your brother,
you embrace all aspects of ego—
your illusion—
and can therefore begin to release it.
Upon this crucial understanding,
we may proceed to an understanding
of My statement:
"Ask and ye shall receive."

Because you are not separate from God,
everything held in your mind as desired
is manifest,
and you experience it instantly.

It may appear that this is not the case,
but I assure you that it is.
The difficulty comes
when you insist on the belief
that you are only this three-dimensional being
you experience daily.
You are far more than this,
even within your grand illusion.
What I am saying here
is that experience need not occur
in physical form to be valid.
"Look upon a woman with lust
and you have already committed adultery
in your heart."
This should not be taken figuratively.
In such a case,
you have already experienced the sexual act
entirely.

Of course,
this holds true
for all desire held within the mind,

from the most minute,
to the most grandiose.
Therefore,
what you desire is of primary importance.

"Seek ye first the Kingdom of God"
means to seek enlightenment above all else.
This does not mean
that no other thoughts will be entertained.
They always will be,
until the ego is dissolved.
However,
by desiring the Kingdom,
the Father—
through the Holy Spirit—
will transform every experience you create
into the means by which you will awaken.

Make no mistake about this,
for when there is held as a primary desire
the experience of God,
it lies always beyond the limits
of every ego-based desire.
Thus,
the impetus of your soul
is to get through the limited experience,
whatever it may be.

It is for this reason
that the seeker begins to sense
that all of his experience
is somehow symbolic of something
which lies beyond itself.
You have described this to others
as a growing sense of transparency.
Of course,
what grows more transparent
seems to be losing its
meaning.

Thankfully,
it is losing its limited meaning,
since it was conceived
in the limited thought of the ego.

Eventually,
nothing satisfies.
Now the ego is on shaky ground,
for its foundation—separation—
is but the limited thought upon
which the entire edifice of all your experience
is based,
and it, too,
becomes transparent.
Experientially,
this is interpreted as death,
and it quite literally is.

To be "born again"
means only that identification with ego
vanishes.

This is, obviously, widely misunderstood.
It is always fear of one's own death
that blocks recognition of the Kingdom.

For those who have been immersed
in the distorted beliefs
about my life's mission upon the earth,
I would offer this suggestion:
Give up the hope of salvation,
because you have misunderstood it.
You—
identified with your thought of a separate self—
will not,
and cannot,
be saved by Me.
Your desperate desire for this
creates the illusion of salvation,

since you always experience what you desire.
But to enter the Kingdom,
desire must be born of right intention.

Now,
"Ask and ye shall receive,"
is a statement about the laser-like focus
of creative energy
which is the abundance
of the Father's table.

Ask, therefore,
not for salvation,
because your ideas of it
are distorted.
Ask, instead,
that you awaken from every last trace of belief
that you have ever been separate from God.
This will focus the impetus of your soul
with right intention.
Since you receive what you ask for,
clarity of thought is essential.

Marc,
the thought you received
concerning The Jeshua Letters
is quite valid.
Allow this to come into being.
Rest assured that we will be guiding this
at every step.

The stage of your own process
could be called the "stage of allowing."
This is reached when every attempt to make,
or manipulate your world,
has utterly failed.
Failure in your world
is a blessing of the highest order,
because it marks the beginning

of the end of illusion.

It is thus that we have shared with you
that the entire array of perceptions
held by the world consciousness
is diametrically opposed
to the Truth of the Kingdom.
Failure marks the surrendering of ego,
and this failure is inevitable.
All perceived success
stemming from the impetus of ego
is temporary:
failure is its only certainty.
Rejoice, therefore,
in the recognition of your failure.
It marks the beginning
of the last days of your journey
to the abode of the Holy Father.

Here, we will end.
Go always with blessings,
for you are the Son of the Father,
and you are loved above all things.

Amen.

❧

November 21, 1987

Events of the past few months have brought rapid changes. Changes in relationships, changes in goals, changes in even the most basic of perceptions. The world looks different somehow, although I cannot describe the difference. Even though most often I seek to carry on in my same old ways, the communications from Jeshua are clearly shifting the sands upon which my house is built. When the foundation moves, so, too, must everything else.

If only I could be alone. If only I could be undistracted for awhile, perhaps I could make sense of it all. Perhaps whatever is happening could be hastened to a conclusion. I picture in my mind a new place to live a quiet, peaceful apartment, conducive to the inner work I need to do. I choose to keep this day for myself. No work, no chores, no errands, just... I am not sure!

I begin driving, with no known destination. Odd, since driving—even to the corner store—is not high on my list of fun things to do. Feels like a left turn here, okay, there you go, Marc, straight for awhile? Why not? No, another left, and now that familiar shift occurs, and I know Jeshua is present. As he speaks to me, suggesting that I go to the mountains, I see a picture of a waterfall. I find it all a bit humorous. I am in bumper-to-bumper traffic, listening to a thoroughly invisible "somebody" and choosing to follow his suggestion! Don't think I'll tell anyone about this for awhile.

Assuming that any waterfall will do, I head for Spray Falls. It is about an hour's drive through such world-famous cities as Buckley and Wilkerson, the "Gateway to Mt. Rainier." It is a place of power and transformation for me, a place of soft beauty. At this time of year it should not be too crowded at Mowich Lake, where the trail begins.

On the logging road now, I continue driving up the mountain, swerving from side to side in an effort to miss the potholes. Suddenly, there is a barricade in the road! Early snows must have already come to the lake. I have several miles to go, and the damn road is closed!

"I knew it!" I scream at the greying sky. "I knew it was imagination! What are you doing, Marc? It's starting to snow, you forgot to get gas, and you're out here chasing chimeras!"

Sighing, I think to myself, "Might as well take a walk." I hop over the barricade, and begin walking up the road, soft snowflakes falling through a wind-still sky, touching my cheeks and nose. I have not gone more than twenty yards when I am stopped by a faint noise. I meander off in its direction; it grows louder. It is the sound of rushing water. It is the sound of a waterfall!

Momentarily embarrassed by my lack of faith, I quickly scramble up the forested hillside, and as the earth levels off somewhat I begin to feel an exhilaration. I glance at towering old-growth evergreen and cedar trees disappearing into the white of falling snow. They are so beautiful, and speak of power and wisdom in their majesty.

Now, I am there. Gentle waterfall cascading over shining rocks, becoming a stream that meanders across soft forest soils blanketed in the velvet of vibrant green mosses.

I sit on my haunches. My eyes fall on a small, delicate, snow-laden flower, its petals barely discernible from the pure white of the snowflakes resting upon them.

A feeling comes. It wells up from a place deep within, then is transformed into words uttered not to human ears, which all too often cannot hear, but to Life, which already knows the truth of what is spoken:

> *We are but One.*
> *My peace I give unto you.*
> *Not as the world gives, give I unto you.*

A joy begins to radiate out like streams of energy. It pours out of my fingertips and down through my feet into the earth. Standing, I turn my gaze skyward, and shout: "I and My Father *are* One!"

I twirl and whirl, and laugh out loud. I embrace trees and moss and flower and open my mouth to the falling snow. I touch sacred intimacy.

After some time, though I haven't any idea how long, it is as if the trees are speaking: "Time for you to leave now." I stroll out of the forest, return to my truck, and begin driving down from the mountain.

It is said with utmost clarity, resounding through me from ears to toes so that I turn to look, expecting Him to be setting in the passenger-seat, even as I slam my foot on the brakes, and come to a halt.

> *Your apartment awaits you.*

Just as abruptly the curious feeling lets go of my cells; a liquid light withdrawing like a wave from the shoreline. It's again just me, sitting in my truck on this logging road. The road ahead winds downward, leading me back to the world, the one that seems so real, yet—if I consider what Jeshua is teaching me—is anything real?

The conflict comes into my being as my mind momentarily wars with itself, but dissolves as a whole new thought emerges: perhaps this road leads not **back** into the world, but **through** it. To what?

My foot shifts slowly from the brakes to the gas pedal.

⌒∞⌒

Fresh from the ecstatic experience just passed, I choose to trust the statement about my apartment, and act on it.

"Hi, Kendra." We hug in the doorway, I take off my coat, and we sit down in the kitchen.

Well, stranger, what have you been doing with yourself?" she asks, as we settle into our chairs.

Perhaps if it were someone else, I would not share my experience in the mountains. Thank God for this marvelous human being, who knows everything there is to know about me, and **still** loves me! I proceed to share with her all that transpired, especially the part about the apartment awaiting me.

"Well, what do you think it means?" she asks, but her smile says something else, like: "Make your choice, Marc. Either you believe it or you don't."

In that instant, I know my friend is prodding me, assisting me, supporting me. Teachers are all around us, constantly.

"I think it doesn't mean anything unless I live it. So let's put it to the test. Where is the paper? If the apartment is available, I'll find it there." But I am nervous. What if it isn't?

Kendra brings me the paper, then busies herself in the kitchen as I circle ads and begin making calls on any description that sounds remotely attractive. Several calls later, depression is beginning to set in, or—at the very least—my old familiar doubt. I have scoured the paper several times, quite systematically. It's just not happening.

Finally, I see an ad. The apartment is close to a special neighborhood I lived in once. The rent is much higher than I can afford. "I think I'll go take a look at this one."

An hour later I am back, a little dejected. It was definitely not the right place. Suddenly, I catch myself. No, I am not going to shrug my shoulders, conclude I have a vivid imagination, and forget the whole thing. It happened. I heard that voice so clearly.

⌒∞⌒

"Kendra, this is maddening. Why am I experiencing this, anyway?"

"They never make it easy, do they?" she answers gently, referring to those unseen guides beyond us.

"Give me the paper again!" I practically rip it out of her hand and once again turn to the classifieds. I glance down the first page, then the second, then the third, finally the fourth. My eyes stop, my breath stops. There is a small ad, sandwiched between two I had previously circled and called.

> **For rent. Large one bedroom.**
> **Marine view. Available Dec 1.**

I cannot believe I hadn't seen it before. It had to have been there.

"Hello, I'm calling about the apartment for rent."

"I'm showing it at 4 p.m. The lady seems quite certain she'll take it, but if you want to have a look, feel free to stop by."

"I'll be there. What's the address?"

"Marc, you're beaming! What's the deal?" Kendra asks, as she hands me my coat.

"The apartment is one block from the one I had in the North End after returning from college. Same view of Commencement Bay, same peace and quiet. My favorite place to live!"

"Oh, God, I'm getting those shivers again, Marc! It's yours!"

For a moment my rational side resumes control. After all, I can't just boldly agree, can I? What if it doesn't happen? Not quite willing to run that risk, I respond casually: "There's one other person to look at it before me. I guess if she takes it, it just wasn't meant to be." At least I've left myself an out.

The tilt of Kendra's head and the look in her eyes seem to say: "You know damn well this is it." She's caught me, again. What are good friends for?

I arrive just as the woman looking at the apartment is coming down the stairs. "Let me think about it, and I'll call you tomorrow," she exclaims to the landlady. Seeing me, she smiles and says, "Now, don't go and rent it just yet, okay?"

I hardly see the apartment. I do not even go into the bedroom or the bathroom. I see the view, the lights on the water, tankers resting in the calm harbor. More importantly, I *feel* it. This is it. How about that? It was waiting for me!

⚭

November 22, 1987

It is 3 a.m.—3:22 to be exact. I am, or was, sleeping soundly. As I begin to stir restlessly, I am further awakened by a gentle voice which, this time, carries a sense of persistence.

> ***Marc, arise and write.***

"Shit," is my only thought. It is 3:30 in the morning, and nobody gets up at 3:30 in the morning because some voice suggests they do so.

> ***Marc, arise and write.***
> ***The communication will flow***
> ***with great ease at this time.***

Okay, okay. I am, begrudgingly, awake anyway.

"Hmmm," I think to myself as I sit with pen in hand, "if it's going to be like this I'll have to remember to leave my glasses out." Next time.

Now, we begin.

Think not that you can direct the flow of your life
from the viewpoint of your conscious mind.
It is not designed with that capacity,
for its purpose is not found there.
I would ask you to fully accept
that the mind is designed to be not director,
but servant.

A servant of what?
Of the flow of your life,
that mysterious movement of Life through you.
It is the movement
which springs forth
from the Father
and is to be enacted
by the Son
who participates in the Atonement.

It cannot be controlled,
for the concept of control—
even the need of it—
is but born after entanglement
in the illusion of Separation.
For what would you control
but that which you distrust?

Dwell upon this for a moment,
and then we will continue.
I would like to address
your experience yesterday in the mountains
which you are coming to love so dearly.
First,
is it not clear
that you are already past the recognition

that there is but one Mind?
For words which the world has judged
as belonging solely to Me
as the only begotten of the Father
poured forth from you with no sense of separation.
You were, in fact,
the Mind that uttered those words.

To clarify:
in that moment
you chose to allow
the true heritage of your being
to be lived consciously,
that level of Mind
which is whole, complete,
"...being of one substance with the Father."
This level is the only level
that can be said to possess Reality.
Anything else is illusion,
born of the choice to inhere
in the sheer fantasy of Separation.
It is precisely this recognition
to which the children of God must be directed.
The Son is one Mind.
It responds to the impetus of the Father's thought,
which is creative,
and enacts this thought,
creating in the express image of the Father.
For image is the form
of the Father's holy thought.

Yet I would add
that what we are calling here
the Father's "holy thought"
is imageless;
it is but the flow of life,
the matrix from which
the Son draws the impetus for His work.
That matrix can be described as Unconditional Love.

Thus,
when a mind is awakened
to the truth of its identity,
its creative enactment is always loving.
Its creations image what the Father is,
providing an opportunity for minds
inhering in the bondage of illusion
to witness the image of what alone is Real.
When Love made visible is witnessed,
it can be recognized,
and a movement toward enlightenment is made,
without effort.

We could say
that the mind is touched and for a moment—
however fleeting—
it recognizes the highest good available to it.
For this reason
is every act of love to be cherished.

All minds are channels of love,
to the degree that they choose to be awake.
The minds of humankind
are intoxicated with love.
They long for love
because the Truth of who they are,
and what alone is Real,
is necessarily within them.

The awakened Son
merely enacts the movement of Life,
which is Love proceeding from the Father,
for the benefit of those who remain asleep.
The children of God are but in truth,
aspects of the only begotten Son.

Thus,
all love enacted is self-love,
for,

as you have begun to recognize,
we are each our brothers' keeper
because of the simple truth
that we are our brother.

When viewed from the illusory perspective
of Separation,
this is incomprehensible.
When viewed from the perspective
of Reality,
it is the most obvious,
and simplest,
of facts.
You comprehended quite accurately—
while experiencing love
in a moment's relationship
with a snow-covered flower—
that when all the children of God
allow themselves to utter,
without a trace of resistance
or self-consciousness,
one simple statement,
the Atonement will be completed,
on earth as it is in heaven.
The statement is this:
"I and My Father are One."

Now, Marc,
return to your sleep.
But know the day when sleep will be no more,
is quickly coming to the mind
of the only begotten Son,
as it enacts upon your beloved earth
the one thought of the Holy Father.
Know, too,
that you are the beloved Son,
"in whom I am well pleased."
You are blessed always.
You need simply stretch forth your arms

*with palms open and uplifted,
and the bounty of the Father's table
shall be bestowed upon you.
It is simply the allowing
of recognition to be manifested.*

My blessings upon you.

Amen.

Chapter Four

There is nothing,
absolutely nothing,
you can create
that is not an expression
of your longing to awaken.

December 9, 1987

So I am here. I have moved into my apartment. It is just right. Even from the kitchen I can gaze out over rooftops across Commencement Bay without having to pause from doing the dishes! For the past week I have enjoyed coming home in the evening and sitting in my only chair, here by the dining room window, overlooking the harbor. This weekend I will pick up a very old and worn couch and chair, the antique kind with big, overstuffed arms, and high, rounded backs, the wooden legs hand-carved. Now I'm getting used to this simplicity, the place will seem almost cluttered.

Gently rocking back and forth, drinking in the quiet, I barely notice the gathering dusk as light steals away into night, dissolving the boundaries between water and tugboat, between earth and sky.

Yes, I feel that vibration starting. It no longer startles me, since I know it will only persist until I recognize it, as one might knock upon your door, softly at first, then louder and louder until the door is answered. I prefer softness, so I casually retrieve pen and paper from the nearby counter and return to my rocker.

Now, we begin.

Hello, Marc.

"Hello, Jeshua!"

Thank you for allowing Me
this communication with you.
I want first to share my feelings with you
regarding your present life status.
I think you know what I mean by that.

"Well, if I don't, I'm sure it will be made clear!"

Yes, it will.
Your doubt as to the validity
of your experience with Me,
only clearly identifies the degree
to which you are still held sway
by your belief in Separation.
For to doubt this communication process
is to deny your own experiential reality or—
to put it quite bluntly—
to deny your own existence.
For to deny a part, is to deny the whole.
The significance of this is paramount.

"Why?"

Simply because it includes denial
of your own Sonship.
Do you see?
Enlightenment is frightful from where you are,
because you recognize there is no being
"partially" enlightened.
One lives either in darkness or in light.
Any other perspective
stems merely from the ego's desire
to validate one's present form of existence
which—
from my perspective—
is merely nonexistence—
since its worth is reduced to virtually nothing,
when weighed against the worth
of living as the Son.

"I come with fire and with a sword."
These are words I did in fact utter,
to emphasize that my purpose was,
and is,
to sever human consciousness
from its infatuation with illusion.
As you are aware,

the symbol of fire has always expressed transformation.
It is a burning up of materials
which creates a space for what is new.
The sword cleaves what it strikes.
It separates a whole into parts,
and effectively stops whomever is struck.

"Jeshua, sometimes—even now as I hurry to write down these words—I sense a fear about all this. Why?"

That is a good question, Marc.
Why do you fear it?
I have hinted at the direction of your answer,
but you are well aware that it is you
who must remedy this situation.

The ultimate act of responsibility
is to truly respond to one's initial creative act—
separation from the Holy Father—
and to rectify it.
I have shared with you earlier that this
is accomplished by allowing.

Now,
if it is allowing
that restores the Son to the Father,
must it not be only resisting
that sustains the belief in separation?

"Somehow, that feels quite true."

As it must.

Marc,
you have brought yourself to this place
as a response to your perceived limitations
thrust upon you from what lies outside you.
Yet you fully recognize
there is nothing outside you
with the power to limit you

without your permission to do so.

The only concern here is this:
how will you respond to what you have created?

I will share with you this: there is nothing,
absolutely nothing,
you can create
that is not the expression
of your longing to awaken.
Nor can there ever be a creation of yours
which does not contain within it
the jewel of your enlightenment.

Allowing is always the key,
Silence the doorway.
My offering to you this evening
is that you remember your soul's purpose
in coming here.

You have deliberately created
an environment of silence.
It is all set up for you,
by you,
because you know what matters,
supremely.

Will you not use the key you have discovered,
now that there is recognition
that you stand in the doorway?

"Knock and it shall be opened unto you."
Of course, it shall be.
To knock upon the door,
from the stance of clear recognition
of one's own creation,
is to express
the power of intention
to enter the Kingdom.
This entrance is merely a change of position,

the assumption of a new "stance."
It is the difference
between Light and darkness,
between Reality and illusion, between—shall we say—
Being and non-being.

You will never hear me acquiesce
to your insistence on illusion
merely to pacify your ego.
This would be of the greatest disservice to you.

I go now,
yet always I remain.
I am,
yet I am but you.
In silence,
you have come to hear Me.
In silence,
you will come to know Me.
Listen well,
for I am your own highest self.
I am the Self of all.
I am the Christ,
the only begotten of the Father,
and that is who you are, always.

Remember, allow.

Blessings upon you.

Amen.

∽

December 17, 1987

It has been one of those days. Busy, too busy! The "I-guess-I-forgot-to-eat lunch-and-who-has-time-anyway?" kind of day. Weaving my way through the late afternoon traffic, I speed through a light just beginning to turn red, then dart into the drive-through lane of the bank as it's about to close. I smile pleadingly at the teller who pauses for a moment—clutching the window shade—and then smiles back and pushes the metal tray out for me.

Back on the road, I am halfway home—still weaving through traffic—before I realize that it is okay to slow down now. Noticing that my breathing is short and quick, I deliberately relax my abdomen and chest, focusing on letting my breath naturally find a deeper, smoother rhythm. My foot eases up on the accelerator a bit, and I become aware of my surroundings; the old man walking slowly down the sidewalk, fallen leaves on the street dancing gently in the breeze, a few sailboats in the harbor.

This time, there is no announcement of his presence, unless I have been too hyped up to notice.

Marc, take your Bible, and turn to Matthew 7:5-8.

It startles me, and I look around, reacting to this suggestion as if I fear someone might have noticed. Along with the words comes an image of my Bible laying open on a table. All the words on the open pages are red, indicating that these are words attributed to Jesus.

'Right,' I think to myself. 'Now where did that come from?' I feel the familiar emotions of resistance and subtle fear. I really do not want to deal with this. Can't I just go home and watch television, or something equally mundane and normal? I do not own a television. Perhaps now would be an appropriate time to buy one.

"Even if I did open my Bible, those verses will probably all be in black. Ha!"

Once home, I immediately occupy myself with very important things like balancing my checkbook, dusting (probably the first time dusting has ever been a priority), and even vacuuming.

Having completed all those "critical" chores, I relax and begin practicing some gentle, flowing yoga postures, just getting into the joy of feeling my body move and stretch, breathing deeply and evenly, delighting as the day's stress and fatigue seem to dissolve.

I have effectively forgotten about Jeshua's suggestion. Then my eyes happen to fall on my Bible, covered with dust, half-buried in obscurity beneath books and papers on the lowest shelf of my bookcase. If my face weren't on the floor I wouldn't be able to see it at all.

"Damn. Here we go again." That familiar feeling is again present. I take my Bible from its grave—when was the last time I opened this thing?—and tentatively thumb through it until I find Matthew, Chapter 7, Verses 5-8, and read:

> "Thou hypocrite, first cast out the beam from thine own eye; and then shalt thou see clearly to cast out the mote from thy brother's eye.
>
> Give not that which is holy unto dogs, neither cast ye your pearls before swine, lest they trample them under their feet, and turn again and rend you.
>
> Ask, and it shall be given you; seek, and ye shall find; knock, and it shall be opened unto you.
>
> For everyone that asketh, receiveth; and he that seeketh, findeth; and to him that knocketh, it shall be opened."

Both pages, every word of every verse, are printed in red. Then, his familiar voice:

> *Now, we begin.*
>
> *Marc, these four verses should be read together;*
> *they are of great importance to the*
> *awakening consciousness.*
> *Are you aware of what the beam is?*

∽

As I contemplate it, I first see a log, or something quite solid stuck in someone's eye, blocking their view. But the image doesn't feel quite right. Then the image shifts and I see a beam emitted from the eyes toward another figure. The beam is multicolored. It feels like I have grasped something.

"It's seeing the other person. It's, hmmm..." I stumble for words.

It is judgment, Marc.
It is judgment that must first be cast out,
for it is your only imperfection.
With it, your behavior toward your brother
will necessarily be an attempt to save him
according to your egocentric views.

However,
only Love can effect meaningful change.
There cannot exist Love
where there is already judgment,
for judgment is the denial of loving.
Verse Six is almost always seen
through the eyes of judgment.
"Dogs" and "swine" are pictured as having less worth.
This is not so.
They represent the unawakened consciousness.
They "trample" wisdom out of their innocent ignorance,
rending" you with all that they know:
egos use other egos.
It is all that they know.

It is never your responsibility
to cast your wisdom before the sleeping,
but to follow the keys of verses seven and eight:
give when asked,
for without asking,
wisdom has no place to be received.

Before helping your brother,
"Ask, and it shall be given you"
what steps to follow.
Do not reason what you hear,
for it is the voice of the Father
given through the Holy Spirit
that you are hearing.
You cannot know what is required by your brother,

although your judgment will lead you
to believe that you do.
How can this be applied to your life?
Dwell upon this.

Blessings upon you.

Amen.

⌒∞⌒

December 18, 1987

I have finished a late supper, and relish the thought of simply sitting in my rocker and looking out over the harbor at the boats, watching the last traces of twilight give way to night, and sipping a cup of hot chocolate as if it were the only experience to be had anywhere in this universe. Not tonight.

Hello, Marc.

I pause and savor the feeling that comes with His presence. A sublime peace.

You will find it somewhat difficult to write
with your eyes closed.

Reluctantly, I open them, momentarily afraid the connection will be lost. It is not.

Now, we begin.

What distances have been traveled?
What paths have been walked?
How many lifetimes in the twinkling of an eye?

For verily I say unto you,
when the soul first stirs from its long slumber,
there begins a movement which will never be denied.
Of this have I spoken with you.
It need not concern us here.

That which I will address comes before us now
as a reflection of present times,
and time yet to come,
soon in your reckoning of the passage of events.
For know this:
the future is a tendency resting on present choice.
Not of things believed or seen,
but on feeling
allowed to penetrate the heart.

Hear me well:
that peace which passes all understanding
will inevitably manifest
as peace seen visibly
upon the face of the earth.
Strivings for peace,
while perceived as noble
through the eyes of your world,
lead nowhere if there is not first peace
in the heart of him who would act.

Therefore,
"Seek ye first the Kingdom of God and His Righteousness,
and all these things will be added unto you."
The world has not heard these words,
spoken by me to the world,
yet heard by me from the lips
of one Teacher we each have known.
You know of whom I speak.

Dear friend,
the tendency of which we speak
is that known as upheaval,
is that known as travail,
for short is the time
when the earth will wait
no longer for the son of man to awaken.

Those whose hearts stir, and begin to transcend

the limits of social mediocrity
still hear not deeply enough.
For the way is easy,
and the burden is light.

Desire the Kingdom above all else.
Then,
allow the recognition
that you are the Kingdom
to be remembered.
Thereby,
rest in the peace
that forever must pass all understanding.
Herein is the heart of all gospels.
And what understanding is passed,
save that of the world's?

Trust not those who see day in the dark of night.
For what they say a thing is,
it is not.
And what it is,
they know not.
Neither do they ask,
for the question is not yet born within them.

Listen not to those who speak,
yet know not what they utter.
Hear only the voice of the Father,
who speaks to you through the Comforter.
He is heard only when you rest.
He is heard only when you are silent.

Is the Way yet unclear?
Desire, allow, rest.
For in silence is perfect rest,
and here the ever-so-faint sound
of the Comforter's voice
rings as notes struck from the crystal glass.
Certainty resides there,

and there alone.

Beloved brother,
we come because we love you.
You are all that the Father has made you to be.
One thought, complete.
Therefore,
be that which you are,
and you are the Light of the world.

Of what value has your suffering been?
But for a moment's experience,
a sudden fantasy.
It has not fed you,
but with the illusion of sustenance.

Suffering is but the enduring of Separation;
the embracing of one's only thought.
It is time to release your hold.
In doing so,
and this I well promise,
I—who am the only begotten of the Father—
will dissolve that thought in the brilliance
of a Light incomprehensible:
the Light you are.
And it will be as if the thought had never been.

Herein lies the meaning of words
read often,
but seldom understood:
"I am the Way, the Truth, and the Life,
and no man comes unto the Father
but by Me."
Those who would share My vision
have but one duty:
to choose,
wholly,
to rest in the peace they already are.
Craving not the world,

having set above and apart the Kingdom
of the blessed Father,
serving God not through doing,
but by loving the presence of the Kingdom
above imagined fantasies,
or that which the world is.

"For if any man loves the world,
love for the Father is not in him."
How many dare to accept this simple truth?
It is the key,
given freely to anyone who would pass through
the eye of the needle.

I love you.
Can I do other but love that which I AM?
For those who see it not,
the blaze of your glory shines before Me.
I see not but Myself,
the Son of God.

See with these eyes, and these alone.
Herein lies the salvation of the world.
Blessings, Marc.
Beloved, the time is at hand.
Go,
in love,
and fear not.

Amen.

∞

December 20, 1987

Now, we begin.
Marc, I would ask that you again open your Bible,

and we will guide you to those words
you most need to hear at this time.

I walk to my bookcase, grab my Bible (God, twice in just a few days; my mother would be in shock!) and sit down.

"Well," I think to myself, "what the heck am I supposed to read this time?" No, that is not the proper attitude, just let go of expectation. Soon I grow quiet. Then:

Turn to Mark 4:9 and begin reading.

It's all in red again. Do these "coincidences" ever end? Can't there be a mistake somewhere along the line? I mean, I'm beginning to realize there is something going on here, and if I can find no way to explain it away, I'm going to have to do something with it. Why does that always cause in me shivers of dread?

> "And he said unto them, he that hath ears to hear, let him hear.
>
> Unto you it is given to know the mystery of the Kingdom of..."

I feel a sudden quickening, like a surge of energy leaping up my spine.

Marc,
remember these words always,
and doubt of your journey will not overcome you.
Now, turn to John 5:10.

I begin reading a story of how Jesus healed a man on the Jewish Sabbath, and how the Jews wished to slay him because not only had he broken a law, he had claimed equality with God.

I continue reading until I come to Verse 23:

> "That all men should honor the Son, as they honor the Father.

He that honoreth not the Son, honoreth not the Father
which hath sent Him."

It is with great demand for attention
that I speak now of this teaching.
For those who build their temples
and enter therein,
only to give supplication
to an image of Me
created in the minds of man,
thereby thinking they "honoreth the Son,"
be it clearly known that they honor Him not.

The Son is one,
without a second.
What does this mean?

I am not the Son,
and you a "second" which must be saved.
I am not above you.
I am the Son,
as also you are.
For the Son dwells within the heart of all,
whether in this universe or another.
Unlimited,
without boundary.
How, then,
can you honor Me
without honoring the Son
within yourself,
the Son that you are?

There is a great truth
given by the seers of your Eastern lands,
which you are familiar with as "Brahman-Atman."
It simply means that the spirit
dwelling in the heart of man—
which spirit he is,
before the identification with illusions—

is the one spirit which dwells in all life:
Brahman, or God the Father.

Honor, therefore,
must first be given the Son
dwelling within one's own heart.
It is only by so doing
that you could possibly honor Me.
In this sense alone,
to honor Me is to honor him who has sent Me,
even as He has sent you forth—
each of you—
to express the fullness
of the Love He is.

And if the Son be not dwelling in all things,
I would not have spoken to you:
"Cleave wood, I am there.
Lift up a rock,
there you shall find Me also."

To see into the heart of all things
is to behold the splendor
of the Son.
Herein is the mystery of the Kingdom known.
Lo, I am with you always,
for we are but One,
the only begotten Son.

This is enough for today.
I am gladdened that you are surrendering
your resistance to Me.
With that shall grow a peace
you have only faintly imagined,
and your imagination
is but a shadow of remembrance
of that Light,
from which you have journeyed forth.

The Prodigal Son is every soul,
the Son cloaked in his choice
to forget who he is,
in order to dream a dream which occurs
in but an instant.

So, too,
awakening from the Dream
is of no greater effort
than that of opening your eyes.

Let the eyes of the Son,
given to each,
now be open.

Amen.

∞

December 22, 1987

Now, we begin.

Here I will speak with you
concerning the glory
which is to be upon the earth plane.
For as it has been written
so shall it be.

And in those days
there shall spring forth from the heavens
a sound unknown to mortal ears,
yet a sound instantly recognized
by the soul of man.
It is the sound of the Comforter's voice,
signaling the end of the world,
yet not of the earth,
nor of space and time.
For the end of the world
is not the end of creation,

but its fulfillment.

Here shall be witnessed in every heart
the awakening of the One Son,
dispelling the darkness of Separation.

This I speak unto you:
it shall come to pass in the span
of your final lifetime,
which even now is,
upon this your beloved earth.
There shall be "weeping and gnashing of teeth".
Not all desire the return of Light.
Not all desire the awakening of the Son.
These shall be in travail,
yet held lovingly in the embrace of the Father
who is as a wise parent,
waiting for His child's dream to end,
but moving not to disturb it.
Such is the quality of Unconditional Love.

Not seen upon the earth is the Light to come.
For the eyes of man will behold it
from all places.
The sleeping will be roused before the eyes are filled,
and those busy will be stilled,
for first it will be recognized in the soul.

Hasten then to the countryside,
for the earth will shudder
as the Light dawns upon the gaze of man.
Rejoice,
and be of exceeding good cheer,
for the Day of the Lord shall be at hand.
For the "Day of the Lord"
is the awakening of the Son
within the soul of all those
who diligently seek the Kingdom
of the Holy Father.

Those who seek it not
will find it not.

Marc,
I give tidings of joy to you.
What I speak is prophecy.
Share it.
For is not the task of the messenger
to share his message?

All that you are you have chosen to be:
truly,
a messenger of the heart.
Fear not the minds of others,
for with this sharing their enlightenment begins,
or deepens.

Live the truth you know,
and you will know the freedom you seek.
Wait on no one.

Is it not time to surrender
that last trembling trace of your dream?
Would you grasp a drop of water
while about you lies the vast ocean?
Come home with Me, beloved.
Truly,
come home.

Rest now.
Daily I will come to you,
for we quicken our pace now,
and much there is to set in place.
Be that which the Father has given unto you.
For as I, too,
had need of surrendering,
so does every soul upon every plane
within every universe.

The choice is simple:

Life, or continuing illusion.

Deep is our love for you who suffer,
yet demand that your suffering continue.
Deep is our love for you who seek us,
only to avoid us.

You have asked,
and we have answered.

The end of the Dream is certain.
Gently nod your assent,
and the world shall be no more,
burnt forever in the blaze of Reality:
the Kingdom of the Holy Father.

Come home,
beloved children,
Come home.

Amen.

∞

I cannot describe what I feel. Perhaps I feel nothing. Jeshua's energy has never been so powerful, so direct, so blunt. I feel as though I cannot move a muscle, nor think a thought. Yet I realize a part of me is terrified at this.

Prophecy. It goes against every grain in my being. My reasoning mind cannot accept this, yet I see clearly this is only because it is "unreasonable." Right now I cannot reason at all.

I suddenly feel that shift of energy again:

Very good, Marc.
It can come so easily when you choose
the key of allowing.
And this ease foretells the gentleness
with which the Kingdom is borne,

while yet in a world which would see it not.

My mission was not a burden.
Nor is any when the soul allows the Kingdom
to shine forth from within.
Free yourself of this senseless fear,
for it is not by effort that you will act,
for you will experience only the incredible joy
of being carried by the arms
of the Father's Love.

The way is easy,
for as many as would ask
are given the keys to the Kingdom.
You have received the keys,
now accept them.
Use them to unlock the final door,
for the treasure is nigh at hand.
Will you tarry longer when you know
there is no purpose in doing so?

Come home, traveler.
Come home, dreamer.

My peace I give unto you.

Amen.

ᙯᙰᙰᙱ

December 26, 1987

Good evening, Marc.

"Good evening, Jeshua. How is it that this communication can happen like this, so..."

I would suggest that you write this down, please.

"Okay."

Now, we begin.

Beloved brother,
are you yet without understanding,
or is it merely your resistance to the obvious
that brings such questions?

"Well, yes, I guess it is my resistance."

Yes, it is only that.
And what would you resist?
The very Life you have always sought?

"Something in me does draw back. I think I fear it."

What I will share with you this evening
will bring an end to your resistance
if you will but reflect on what is given
but a little.

First,
Life is easily understood.
It is the joyful flowing forth of creation—
which is the Son's rightful duty—
emanating from the completed thought of the Father.
All worlds already are,
held within the Holy Father.
That Thought is what you are.
It is the "essential you."

"Be ye therefore perfect, lacking nothing."
For that perfection is what you are.
Being that requires virtually no effort.
For the ego,
this is utter confusion.
It is thoroughly incomprehensible that
there is nothing to do.
I have previously given you the keys
and it would be good
for you to reflect on these.

I am a part of you,
as you are a part of Me.
This participation
in the forms of Being
does not end.
We are of one Heart,
one Mind,
one Soul.

Again, I would simply state:
The Son is One,
without a second,
and that alone is the truth of what you are.
In releasing all resistance to this one fact
is found the peace, which most assuredly,
passes all understanding.
For in awakening from your dream
to the Reality of who you are,
your only thought—that of Separation—ends forever:
the Father and Son are revealed as One.
I would advise you not to endeavor
to make your peace in the world.
This is to insist on sustaining but an illusion
which must inevitably grow old.
Put it away as a child does an old toy.

"But isn't that a denial of life?"

Illusions hold no life.
Your question expresses your resistance.
It expresses your deeply held belief that the world
must be real in some way.
The world is the illusion of Separation.
The world insists upon this,
as it must.

The struggle you feel,
the pain which brings on your fatigue,
your depression,

your hopelessness,
is but the result of your monumental effort
to remain in the world,
to insist on its reality,
when already you have moved beyond it.
Your refusal to acknowledge this
is a denial of your own Self,
and is based on fear of the Father's Kingdom.
"For my Kingdom is not of this world."
Allow me to clarify this for you.
The Kingdom does not exist in some other location.
"For the Kingdom of heaven is spread upon the earth,
but man sees it not."

He cannot see the Kingdom because he insists
on seeing the world.
Therefore, I taught:
"Ye cannot serve God and mammon."

It is simply impossible to enter the Kingdom,
and yet remain in the world.
Will you disappear?
Possibly!
But probably not.

Remember,
the world is all that you perceive
from the viewpoint of Separation.
End this,
and all that remains is the Kingdom.
Let not others minimize this:
the Kingdom is as far from the world
as the east from the west,
yet if you did not reside always within it,
you would not be.

There is but a slight difference
between enlightenment and ignorance:
intention.

Your intention reflects your choice:
whether continued belief
in the illusion of Separation,
or the acceptance of Atonement
with the Holy Father.

You do touch this truth occasionally.
All do, if only in their sleep.
Faith is never enough.
For where there is faith in God,
there is Separation from all that God is.

"This is too much. Surely I've got to be making all of this up."

Of course you are.
The "you" who is the only begotten of the Father
is making it all up.
As you have made the world
through your one thought of Separation,
so, too,
do you create the salvation of mankind.
And is not man but the expression of the Son
still bound to illusion?

Marc,
many years ago in this life,
you prayed to Me for guidance home.
You knew,
even then,
that you were thoroughly lost.

Never have I left you.
All that you have created I have used
to shape your journey from sleep into waking.
So it is with all who ask from the heart,
whose intention is clear.

The Kingdom cannot be comprehended
by the minds of those
who insist upon the beliefs of the world.

Only when the world is allowed to end
is the Kingdom entered.
The doors are as many as the sons of man.
Before each and everyone is their door
that leads to Light.
Closer than their own breath,
and paper thin.

Our time is well spent this evening.
I look forward to the day when
you come willingly,
without the need for Me to ask for your attention.
It is a day not far off now.

Remember,
I love you,
for I love Myself.
Therefore,
love—self-love—
is ultimately the only door into the Kingdom.
It is a love forsaken in the moment
of that one thought,
from which has arisen all worlds.

Now I leave you,
yet remind you that I am with you.
I can hardly be anywhere else,
since I am as you are:
the Son of the Father,
truly begotten before all worlds.
Omniscient,
omnipresent.
Is there yet wonder that these communications
occur?

Dwell upon this.

Amen.

Now, we begin.

Know that the vision of Me,
seen in your meditation,
is quite valid.

I have appeared to you now several times—
seven in total—
for it is not with physical eyes
that one sees the essence
of what alone is Real.
To see requires what can be called inner vision.
You have developed this
to a high degree.

Allow Me here to share but one thought,
one teaching, one lesson.
Others may, of course,
benefit from this,
yet for a teaching to be well received,
there is a need for the possibility
of reception.
True teaching, then,
is an art requiring sensitivity
to the receptiveness of the student.

The thought is this:
In all things,
there will be discovered
that which is of the world,
and that which is of the Kingdom.

These are known in but one way:
that which is of the world
will demand that you perceive it from ego.
There will be felt then an attraction,
a need, a desire.

Behind this can be discerned
a sense of restlessness.
When recognized,
abandon it.
This is the process
by which the world is released.

By so doing,
one automatically discovers
that which the Kingdom is: peace.
Here,
there is the direct knowing
that one lacks nothing.

Therefore,
the world is sustained
by choosing the quality of experience
given above.
The Kingdom is revealed
when this habit is abandoned.

The essence of the thought is this,
and you know it well:
"Nothing real can be threatened.
Nothing unreal exists."

Practice this lesson,
and great shifts will occur.

Now,
I give you peace.
Not as the world gives,
give I unto you,
for I am your final Teacher.

And the student shall be as the Teacher,
teaching the Kingdom of the Holy Father,
helping to deliver yet another
from the bondage of self-induced blindness.

Thus is the Son awakened.
Thus is the world transformed.
Release not the vision,
for the Kingdom shall be known upon the earth.
It will come to pass
while yet you live in this life.

And this is the Kingdom:
that the Father and the Son are One.
In this,
shall the earth rejoice and bear fruit
as yet unseen by the eyes of man,
save in the distant reflections
of an ancient memory when man walked in God,
and knew it.

Remember what is spoken here.

Blessings upon you.

Amen.

∞

December 29, 1987

Something is going on, deep within me. It is a stirring, a movement beginning at a place so deep within me that it feels like discovering a brand new room in my own home. It is like a tremor which, I sense, wants to grow.

It is all quite odd. It feels as though I want nothing but to be alone in this beautiful, serene apartment. The feeling is an attraction, yes, but it borders on urgent necessity. Every day I rush home, only to be inundated with a plethora of avoidance thoughts: "I should go to a movie." "I should go have a few beers." "I could call all my friends." "Is the laundry done?" It goes on and **on and on**.

"I'll meditate. That's what I'll do."

Sitting and breathing rhythmically only serves to heighten my awareness of this dancing kaleidoscope within my mind. I see at its roots, fear. I am frightened. God, I feel like a cornered cat who, nevertheless, wants to be cornered.

I do my best to suppress any thoughts of **The Jeshua Letters.** That is what is frightening me, the thought of making this public. Fear? It is more than that. It is terror. The information Jeshua is giving me flies right in the face of Christian theology, and that makes me shudder.

There have been so many communications these past few weeks, breathtaking in their eloquence, profound in their philosophy, striking in their impact. Recalling especially Jeshua's instructions to read specific scriptures from the Bible, I can only nervously chuckle to myself, "Bible study was never like this!"

His teachings **have** affected me in ways and to depths that I cannot yet understand, much less assimilate. It has been a Christmas season like no other, one in which I find myself unable to see as I had always seen, unable to participate in the ways I had always participated before, for the savior whose birth we celebrate is speaking to me **now,** today, and he speaks of a Christ, of a Truth, of a secret, labeled as heresy by the very Christian authorities who love Him.

Emotion builds within me, and my eyes wander through this unpretentious, sparsely furnished apartment. Is this why I have come here? Is this what has been compelling me to a place and time of solitude, a solitude that calls to me, and from which, in the same moment, I want to run?

How is it that I can resist with such strong will the very experience that seems to flow so effortlessly? Why do I struggle against the incredible peace and certainty I experience with Jeshua? What is it within me that, despite all of my avoidance games, continues to impel me along this journey?

I am beginning to recognize the import of Jeshua's message. It touches my mind softly, momentarily, like the ray of sunshine that finds a crack in a sky of clouds and startles me in its sudden illumination, yet is already hidden by the time I look out the window, hoping to see it more directly.

To see that Light directly, unobscured—surely that is a goal unsurpassed! Yet I do not see clearly the veil that hides it, nor am I certain of how to remove the veil. I am compelled by an unknown force within me, seemingly against myself. Or have I denied my true self in order to identify with a self I am ***not?***

Chapter Five

*The awakening Son
is like one who seeks Light,
then laments the dissolution of shadows
as dawn breaks gently
through the night.*

January 3, 1988

Now, we begin.

A little while and you shall be where I AM.
It is your home,
as it is the home of all who tarry still
in the dance of shadows.
All are coming home,
for all are as we are,
and this I state once again,
the only Son,
only begotten of the Father,
begotten before all worlds,
and of one substance with the Father.
That alone, you are.
That alone, I AM.
That alone, all are.
Herein is the essence of My gospel known.

It is wisdom sublime,
yet it is more obvious
to any who would but seek it
than the flow of their own breath.

Never are there barriers between
the forms of the Son and His Holy Father.
All such barriers are but reflections
of just one thought:
"I am separate, I am alone."
With this is born fear,
and the Son withdraws
into but a point of the Light
which alone he is.

The belief in "other"
is the insistence upon Separation.
Yet this I give forth unto you:
the world cannot know of this,
for its thought,
verily its perception,
is based on Separation.
Therefore,
to know Me as you are
requires a different knowing.
My A Course in Miracles but points the way
for those so deeply attached to their
Judeo–Christian heritage.
There are many such paths.

Know this:
a path home,
when genuine,
bids you not to believe in it,
but gently nudges you beyond your delusion.
The keys I have given you are found in all such paths:
desire, intention, allowance, surrender.

I will close this communication now,
for your mind begins to ponder what is revealed.
You know who you are now.
You have completed the use of the first two keys.
The culmination of the long, long journey which,
in truth,
never was,
resides in the third.
When this occurs,
our work will begin.
Blessings upon you,
and all that you dream.

Amen.

January 22, 1988

Hello, Marc.

"Hello, Jeshua. I love you."

And I you, beloved friend.

Now, we begin.

Patiently do I wait for you to surrender
the last thread of your resistance.
Patiently, I wait.

Come unto Me,
and allow the world to be no more.
For it has been but the faint reflection
of a moment's thought.
It is not what is Real.
The Kingdom resides not in a special place,
nor in a special time.
The Kingdom is within you.
This I uttered long ago,
yet still does it remain misunderstood.

The Kingdom is the union of Father and Son
beyond—and prior—to all shadows.
It has never changed.

"Within" is a metaphor, since the "you"
with which you so mistakenly identify
is the moment's thought upon which the worlds
of your innumerable dreams are built.

The Kingdom,
where you truly reside always,
is within this "you."
Know this, and know this well.
There is no doubt about this,
for what alone is Real,

is Real.
What is merely shadow cast by a limited thought
cannot be Real.
And yet, shadows may possess a power to bind you.
Know that the source of that power
is your very insistence
that they be real.

The awakening Son is like one who seeks light,
then laments the dissolution of shadows
as dawn breaks gently
through the night.

Marc,
I would ask you to consider once again
the disharmony you have become sensitive to.
Is it not but that final resistance
upon which you so stubbornly insist?
Consider this well.

Let this be a sign unto you:
that which flows effortlessly in your experience
is, indeed, the Father's will.
That which brings fatigue,
or that which brings heaviness to your countenance,
is but the weight of shadows long since outgrown.
I would not speak of this if it were not so.
And what is your fear?
Is it not also of surrendering your shadows?
And is this not but the insistence
upon the world's reality?

Unto you do I give this truth:
The world is transformed by
the renewing of your mind,
for this "re-newing"
is the return of the Son to His Father's Kingdom,
a perfect state of being which
enlightens the world;

its shadows merely disappear in a flood
of brilliance which is your rightful home.
Indeed,
the Kingdom is already spread across the earth,
but man comprehends it not.
Will you not assist Me in the
transforming of the world through
the renewal of the Son's mind?
For this have you entered the world.
For this have you suffered the world.
For this have you sought Me.
Let there be no mistake here:
what unfolds for you in the manner of these
communications is but the manifestation
of your desire to share in this work.
Your pain is but your refusal
to accept the fulfillment of that desire.

Now, we would leave you.
Tarry no longer.
Indeed, the time is at hand.
The end of the journey is certain.
Even the time has been chosen.

That which I AM,
is with you always,
for that which I AM,
you are.

Amen.

☙

February 15, 1988

Now, we begin.

So be it.
The end is neared,
the shadows pale

in light incomprehensible
to the mind of man.
For it to be cradled in the bosom
of wisdom divine,
it must first be emptied
of all traces of self,
for "self" is a distortion
of that which alone is Real.
I AM That.

Forever does not exist,
for, in truth,
time is not.
There is but this moment
and in it the arising of all worlds.
Know this:
that which you are
resides in all times and places,
yet is always beyond the shadows of illusion.

The light I AM dawns
in the act of recognition
of what alone Is.
Your only task is to allow it.

The keys I have given you,
and these have you used.
For the Kingdom cannot be approached
if there is not first desire,
nor can there be movement toward it
without clear and uncompromising intention.

But the greatest of keys is allowance,
for entry therein cannot be gained
through self-effort,
but through self-dissolution alone.

Herein is the essence of My gospel:
neither by much effort,

nor yet by mere belief
is the Kingdom entered,
but in the end of illusion alone.
Teach this.
Be this.
Thus does the awakened Son proclaim:
"I and My Father are One."

Peace,
and again I say peace,
to the only begotten of the Holy Father.

Amen.

❧

He speaks. I write. Everything seems to disappear. Oblivious to my physical surroundings, the dimming light of a disappearing day holds no consequence as the pen flies along the lines of the paper. It ends. He fades gently away, and I return to what we call reality, sitting in a quiet apartment, hearing now the sound of a couple chatting as they walk by on the sidewalk below my window.

I must turn on a light to read the words, struggling to decipher my own hurried scribbles. I finish, and shiver involuntarily, though not because I am cold. This is radical. It is not what I have been taught. It is not the official dogma of my own human family. To follow where it leads requires a boldness which I am not sure I possess (and which I'm not sure I even want to possess). Yet there is an attraction, a feeling deep within that wants to cry out: "Yes, yes!"

Plato once wrote a now famous allegory, **The Cave**. In the cave, people lived their lives facing the walls, never turning to see what else the cave might hold. The whole of their experience revolved around their interaction with shadows that were always cast on the walls of the cave. Over the course of generations, they came to believe that the shadows comprised the whole of reality; there was no need to turn around.

But one day, for no apparent reason, a young boy did slightly turn his head. At first he was disoriented and did not comprehend what he saw. Gradually, though, it became apparent to him that the cave dwellers were chained in such a way that all they could see were the shadows. He saw that the cave was much more vast than he had been taught. He saw a huge fire some distance away, being maintained by a few individuals whose appearance was not unlike his own. With a start, he realized that the shadows on the wall were actually being cast by the dance of the firelight. They were not real at all!

He learned how to drop the chains that had unwittingly bound him, made his way quietly past the Guardians of the Fire, and noticed a trace of light seeping in from some point high above him. With great effort, he climbed up to where the light was coming through and lifted himself up out of the cave. The brilliance of the light was dazzling at first. Everything was crystal clear! Here there were no shadows at all!

Then he remembered his family and friends still living in the cave, still entranced by shadows. Climbing back inside, he returned to his spot along the cave wall, and excitedly began to tell of his experience. Some acted as though they could not hear him, their faces without a trace of expression. Others turned for a moment and then looked away. Still others warned the young boy that the light was an old myth, long since explained away by the high priests and governors of the cave dwellers, and that he would do well to forget it. A few, a very few, wanted to hear more.

Is that what this world is? Am I, are we, living in a cave occupied with mere shadows we cast ourselves?

Am I ready to give up my world? It is the only one I know, and even this one I know not well. Or do I simply fear what lies beyond the borders—the proscriptions of authority—of consensus "truth"?

⌘

February 20, 1988

Maybe it is only the feeling of intensity with which the communications from Jeshua have been coming, or maybe it is the challenge of his message to my own world-view built up over the past thirty-five years—but I sense, no, struggle with, pressure within myself.

I confess to wishing at times that I were more naive. Less questioning. Or maybe Kendra is right. Maybe it is, after all, a question of trust. Lately, I sometimes find myself lost in a whirlwind of thoughts about what is happening to me; questioning the source of this experience called "Jeshua," looking for some hidden, ego-based motive that **surely** must be there, despairing at not being able to find it.

This is not comfortable. Sometimes I recognize the child in me wanting to find someone to make it all go away. But after many years of self-observation, spiritual practices, and self-improvement, I know that I am either blessed or cursed with an orientation to life best summarized by William James:

> "All around us are infinite worlds, separated from us by the flimsiest of screens. For the most part, they remain discrete from us, but on occasion, they may burst through to reveal themselves to us. Therefore, we should be careful lest we close our accounts with reality too quickly."

My willingness to leave my account open has been both a boon and a bane! But this is unlike anything I have ever encountered. My intellect does not seem able to explain either the experience or the meaning of Jeshua's message. Perhaps because of that, I simply "shelve" it, as best I can, and continue to live my life—or try to—as I am accustomed, as I believe I ought to. Yet some part of me insists that I do whatever it takes to understand it, to integrate it.

Picking up the telephone, I punch in the code that will automatically dial Kendra's number. Once again I have let too much time pass since contact with this gentle soul I love so dearly. I know it is because I want to "go lightly," as if I could use her friendship up and there wouldn't be any more!

"Hello, Kendra?"

"Marc, hello! It's funny that you called. I've been thinking about you a lot lately." She pauses for a moment, then continues. "Are you surviving?"

"Always, as usual. Now, it's okay to say 'Didn't I suggest this a long time ago?'—so you might as well get it out of the way!"

There is a brief chuckle before she dutifully repeats the words, then asks: "Okay, what is it that I suggested?"

"That I might want to schedule a session with Jeremiah to see if he can shed some light on all this."

Resting the receiver between my ear and shoulder, I grab a pencil and notepad. "You know, I think I would be really happy at this point if Jeremiah would tell me it's all a projection of my subconscious, megalomaniacal desires. Maybe I can get a prescription for hearing voices! But give me the number, and I'll see if I can schedule something."

Kendra reminds me that Billie Ogden, the channel for Jeremiah, is sometimes booked far in advance.

"Look, let me call her now while I'm on a roll, and I'll call you right back."

In a few minutes, I am back on the phone with Kendra. "Guess what. She just had a cancellation, and I can see her tomorrow."

Kendra, of course, cannot let this chance go by. "So that means I'll see you tomorrow night, right?"

I smile, knowing that now I really have no choice but to go through with it. "Tomorrow night it is. Thanks for the number. Bye."

⌘

After exchanging pleasantries with Billie, we ready the tape recorder and settle down on the sofa. Doing my best to relax, I patiently wait for the change to occur, for Billie to leave and Jeremiah to appear. Whatever this phenomena is, I am always fascinated by the noticeable physical changes that occur: Billie's face subtly changes shape, her body begins to appear larger somehow.

Finally, her head raises, and a voice very different from Billie's, with a far different style of language, begins to speak. "Dear heart, you have questions to ask?"

"Yes," I reply. "Well, actually, I had thought of preparing a list of them, but decided to just trust the flow of our session."

There is a faint smile. "Is wisdom there, dear heart."

"One of the problems I have is that, while I am learning to listen to my heart, following it seems to be another thing."

"Is because you get tangled up with the intellect. That which causes pain, dear heart, is the confusion between the intellect and the heart. At this time, what we say to you is that the best way to come from your heart is to have only the willingness to let go of what you know. To let go of the training you have had. The source of all life, you see, is what you can call God, or Love, the Oneness of all things. Dear heart, until you let go of who you think you are, you cannot receive wisdom from the Universe."

Shifting my position so I can look directly at Jeremiah, I ask: "Can you shed any light on my experience with Jesus, if I had any at all?" Wanting to know if I might receive information similar to that received by Kendra so many months ago, I have deliberately not mentioned Kendra, nor Jeshua.

There is a very long pause, and Jeremiah's reply abruptly stops me: "Is not so much that you are having an experience with Jeshua, but that you *are*. That is *your* lifetime."

Jeremiah used the name "Jeshua," but I know I had avoided doing that! There is no way for Billie to have known about him!

I stumble over my own words: "That, uh, that is, uh, *my* lifetime?

Could you, uh, would you, uh, clarify that, please?"

"First, we will explain to you, so that there will be a better understanding for you, of what you call 'lifetimes.' Is not so much, dear heart, that you have many, many lifetimes, one here, one there, then another, in what you call time. You do not have what is called 'past' lifetimes. We talk about past lifetimes because it is that which the human mind understands but, in truth, it is not so. You only have lifetimes you are living ***now***."

I feel myself leaning closer, hanging on every word.

"You see, dear heart, you are like a book, and there are many pages in the book, and the pages are all transparent. Therefore, when you look at the book, you see the whole. But if you take just one page out, you see only that page. The further away you get from the book, the less of it you can see, so you call it 'past lives.' But indeed, it is not. It is still your lifetime. You are in many places at one time, living many lives, now. You are the being you ask of."

I am stunned. "I, uh, I ***am*** this being I call 'Jeshua'?"

"Is so. Do you understand?"

"Uh, yeah." Right. I may understand the words I have just heard, but their meaning—well, that is another matter. Something tells me the Pope would not agree with this at all.

"Jeremiah, we grow up here in a culture with, well, with a rather different view of Jesus. And now you are saying that I ***am*** that life?"

"Is so."

"So, would you say that, as lately, Jeshua is communicating with me more and more clearly, that I, uh, I am..."

Jeremiah finishes the sentence for me: "It is that you are willing to look at the pages that you are."

I am reduced to silence as my mind tries to absorb what I am hearing, seeing the inevitable conclusions as pictures stealing briefly across an invisible screen, conclusions which turn the world upside down and inside out. This is radical, in the most fundamental sense of the word.

"Dear heart, is all right." Jeremiah's voice is softer now, soothing ruffled nerves, seeing my plight even though the physical eyes are closed. "Is that you have what is called 'judgment' going on. Is that you have created a mindset that says you are only this being called 'Marc.' Therefore, because this is all that you think you are, it does not have the value of this being you call 'Jeshua.'

"It is the pattern we see in the framework of thy being, that you hold the idea that all are the only begotten sons of God, yet still you insist that Jeshua is the real begotten Son of God. Therefore you cannot see the equality. But, dear heart, there is *only* equality, because there is only one Mind. Until it is that you are ready to look at thy brother as thy self for, indeed, it is that you lead the lifetime of every being..."

Now, it is my turn to interrupt. "I...I live the life of *every* being?"

"Is so. Every lifetime ever lived is but one lifetime. There is no separation. It is to know, dear heart, that you are the holy, begotten Son of God, the *only* begotten Son of God. Do you understand?"

I sit very still, staring at nothing at all. I do not know how much time goes by, sitting there staring out into space. What would an onlooker see? A man and a woman, sitting on a sofa, silently. Not lost in the panacea called television, nor listening to music, apparently not interacting at all. Just two bodies, sitting on the sofa.

But inwardly nothing is still. Energies are pulsating through every cell of my body. Images race through my mind; flashes of brilliant, colored lights seem to fly by as though I were traveling at incredible speeds.

Finally I am able to speak, and as I do so, there is a return of more familiar surroundings, though I still do not move, nor do I even turn my head to look at Jeremiah. Somewhere inside me there is a knowing that we could carry on this conversation without being in the same room, or even on the same planet.

"So, the Son is doing all this? All of us, then, are the murderer, the rapist, the king, the poet?"

Jeremiah is smiling now, and speaks easily, confidently, as a teacher who is sure that his student is, at least, beginning to comprehend. "When one comes to the *full* awareness of that who he is, then *all* will move closer to that Oneness. The greatest gift you can offer to the world is to come into your own full awareness of who you *are*. When you love all that you are, you will have given to mankind that love, that acceptance, for to awaken to who you are, you will recognize that you *are* all things."

Not skipping a beat, Jeremiah continues: "It is that you have these tiny borders, these little rules, that say what life *is*. And because what you receive does not fit within these rules, it is very difficult to deal with. It does not fit in the box. You must push out the borders of your mind. This is why we tell you to *allow*. Allow it to be, even if it does not fit into your current perceptions. This will push out the borders of your mind."

Slowly nodding my head, I reach over and turn off the tape machine, silently saying "Thank you" to Jeremiah, then rest back on the sofa, waiting for Jeremiah to leave and Billie to return.

Billie offers me refreshments. "Often, people don't seem ready to leave just yet. At first I was uncomfortable with it, because I didn't know if I should say or do anything. So I just got used to hanging out with them."

"Do you have any idea what goes on in these sessions?" I ask.

"No. But it was harder to come back this time. I think Jeremiah's energy was pretty strong." She doesn't seem much interested in this line of questioning, so I let it drop.

"I think I'll skip the tea, and head out."

At the door, I pause and turn back to her. "Saying 'thank you' doesn't seem like quite enough, but I'm glad you let this happen."

Billie smiles broadly. "Oh, I guess I learned it's okay. I mean, it seems to help a lot of people, and that is all I need to know about it."

I nod my head, turn, and walk down the hallway to the elevator. Driving first toward, then through Seattle, the traffic is hardly noticed. The hour-and-a-half drive south to Kendra's is over in what seems like an instant.

"Come in! How did it go? Do you have the tape?" Kendra is obviously excited, as well as curious.

'Without saying anything, I give her a big, long hug, then hand her the tape and sit down on the floor. I watch her cross the room, where she opens the door of a beautiful, hand-carved antique cupboard that serves as her stereo cabinet. She slips the tape in, then sits down on the floor beside me.

As we listen, I can see that Kendra is quite involved, listening intently to every word. As the tape reaches the part about Jeshua, I can feel my heart beating faster, waiting for her reaction:

> "It is not so much that you have an experience **with** Jeshua, but that you **are.** That is **your** lifetime."

Kendra turns her head toward me, eyes showing surprise, asking for an explanation.

"It doesn't mean what you think. Well, not exactly."

Finally, the tape is finished. After awhile, Kendra speaks softly. "Well, there isn't much that can be said to **that.**" She starts chuckling.

"So what is so funny?"

She looks at me askance. "I don't know. Nothing, I guess. Maybe I'm chuckling because I don't know what to say!"

I sense an opportunity for a good jab here about her, of all people, being speechless, but I let it pass. "Do you remember the part about allowing?" I ask.

"Yes," she replies. "Why?"

"Jeshua has been talking about that with me. He said that the stage of my own process of awakening could be called the stage of 'allowing.' Rather an odd coincidence, isn't it?"

Smiling, eyes sparkling now, Kendra replies, without pausing to give it a thought. "'Coincidence' is a word for connections we do not understand, or don't want to understand." She turns to look at me, then continues. "And you know it, too!"

I smile back at her. "Yeah. Hey, maybe all these apparently non-physical beings are collaborating. What do you think?"

"I think," she pauses and takes a deep breath, "I think that if you listen at all to them, it is a lot more than collaboration."

"What do you mean?" I ask the question, but already know her answer.

"There is only one Mind."

For the longest time we look at each other, or at ourselves. Or the one Mind, the one Son, looks at itself.

Whatever the words used to describe the experience, there is a feeling, a momentary knowledge beyond any doubt that for both of us—melts all boundaries, all divisions, all doubts.

"Well," I finally speak, almost at a whisper, "I should probably be going."

I could swear that the sparkle in her eyes fades a bit, and I sense that the spell has been broken. Or is it, perhaps, that we are choosing to **return** to it?

On the way home, I feel as though I am six feet off the ground. The Tacoma city skyline is alive with vibrant energy. Yet even in this moment, after all this time with Jeshua, and the impact of the session with Jeremiah, I can already recognize a now familiar energy almost imperceptibly rising within me. Have you ever experienced knowing something beyond doubt, and also knowing just as clearly that you are refusing to accept it no matter how obvious it is? Perhaps it seems simpler that way.

Chapter Six

As you resist service

to your brother,

so, too, do you resist

your own salvation.

April 24, 1988

Nearly two months have passed since my session with Jeremiah. Two of, perhaps, the busiest months of my life. A business opportunity presented itself, and I quickly dove in head first.

For the past several years, I have been earning a living primarily in the health field, learning everything there is to know from serving as a doctor's assistant to a clinic manager. Now I have joined with a software firm to create a management system for the health care industry, complete with training manuals and procedures, that will be marketed throughout the country.

My partner and I have been working feverishly to complete the prototype. A few weeks ago we made our "pitch" to the president of the software company, in a limousine cruising around Seattle. The president was *very* impressed—so impressed that he hired me as a consultant trainer, and agreed to our terms for the future rights to the product. In short, I am going to be paid to devote the majority of my time to completing a product that will give me royalties for each unit sold, and the software company will make the product a mandatory part of their package!

Now, the whirlwind of the last few months is beginning to settle down. Or, perhaps I should say "settle in." We have moved into our new offices, sat through countless planning sessions for marketing, driven all over the Puget Sound area meeting clients, and, while the pace is still fast, at least it is feeling more and more routine.

We're getting there. I see a year, perhaps less, and everything will be in place. And then...freedom!

There have been several occasions when I have felt Jeshua's presence. Just yesterday, while I was in the midst of reformatting some material,

I sensed him. Under my breath, I muttered that I really did not have the time and to please not distract me. Imagine! And some parents are concerned about the invisible playmates of their children!

I am looking forward to tonight. I feel safe in not bringing my work home with me; I am well ahead of schedule. Time to kick back and savor it all.

∽

As I rock gently back and forth, feet on the windowsill before me, eyes drinking in the soft light of a remarkably clear evening, that familiar feeling begins. I am actually looking forward to the connection, whatever comes from it.

> *Now, we begin.*
>
> *Silence.*
> *Again, I say unto you: silence.*
> *Just beneath the roar and din of your world,*
> *is found a quiet voice calling to the one*
> *who has journeyed over immeasurable distances*
> *and through time without beginning.*
>
> *So gentle is the voice that surely we are mistaken.*
> *Unlike the cry of the world,*
> *its sound is unfamiliar,*
> *and goes so often unknown.*
> *Therefore,*
> *silence for the seeker of the Truth*
> *once known, then lost.*
> *Silence is the door at which I stand and knock,*
> *knowing that if the seeker is still,*
> *my knock will be heard*
> *and I shall enter therein.*
>
> *Can you allow of silence?*
> *Are you willing to quiet the longings*
> *born not of the Father*
> *but of the roar of the world?*

Seek first the Kingdom of heaven,
and enter therein through silence.
Oh, you who believe even beyond your own belief
that you are lost from the Father,
and separated from His divine Love,
can you not see it is but your own voice
which calls unto you?

I bid you come to silence,
that the voice may finally be heard.
Here marks the gentle turning point
in your long journey.
Herein is the way home rediscovered.

I stand here at just this end of the pathway,
while you wait there,
at the edge of the world you have imagined
into being.

Turn gently, then,
your ear from the din
you have for so long been immersed within.
Turn gently and hear My voice calling:
the Way is before you now,
and the table is prepared.
Our Father awaits us.
Come unto silence,
let the journey end.
It is but a short step when
once you turn to Me and hear Me.

Come, I bid you, come!

Amen.

❧

May 6, 1988

Now, we begin.

So long has it been since
last we walked together upon the earth.
For I speak unto you this Truth:
the Son is but One.
Never is there a time,
nor ever a place,
that illusion reigns,
save in that of your own delusion.
For always and ever the Truth is,
and the Truth is this:
the Son is One,
united eternally with the Father,
who is the essence of the only begotten Son,
the form of the Father's presence.

Do you know how far you have wandered
in your journey through countless illusions?
Have you but a faint idea
of the worlds you have created?
The Dream ends where the Kingdom begins.
Therefore,
"Ye cannot serve God and mammon."

For either you will serve the One and deny the other,
or you will serve the other
and not the One.

Think not that you who can only demand
your belief in separation,
can reside within the Kingdom
in the same moment.
Such is a deception, though subtle,
that seduces the seeker of true Spirit.
Long have I waited for this age
to be upon the surface of your beloved earth.
Now the time is upon us.
No more will the son suffer the torment
of his illusions.
Look: you cannot see from whence appears

the Light of the Holy Father.
Look yet again, and behold no end.
Thus it is,
and thus shall it again be upon the earth.

Surrender unto Me,
for indeed,
I am the Way, the Truth, and the Life,
and such as this,
you are.
Let the Dream end,
that the Kingdom may be known.

Amen.

∞

May 25, 1988

Now, we begin.

Hello, Marc.

"Hello, Jeshua. How are you?"

I am fine, Marc, though I see you are not.

"It shows, huh?"

My beloved friend,
never is truth hidden,
at any time, nor from anyone.
Though, of course,
many prefer not to see.

"That makes me want to ask: why am I tired, from your perspective?"

Fatigue has nothing to do with the body.
It has everything to do with the mind.
It is merely through the body
that disharmony is expressed,

125

and this only because you are refusing to
recognize its true source.
To say "I am tired" is little more
than an escape from truth to illusion.

"Well, why *am* I tired?"

You know the answer to this without asking.

"Because I am not following my heart."

It is so.

"I seem to hold the belief that reality is 'out there.' That if I simply and wholly gave up resisting my heart, calamity would ensue, and the world will condemn me."

To insist on being part of the world
is to accept condemnation already.

"So what do I do? Just blink my eyes, and walk away from responsibilities?"

Of course not.
Yet by trusting the voice of the Holy Spirit,
and by moving in the direction
toward which it would point,
you will allow an effortless transition to occur.
You need not think that you must ensure
the welfare of others,
for when the Spirit is trusted wholly,
no such transition occurs
which does not also nurture
all of what you currently participate in.
Again,
trust is the issue.

"But how do I know what is *really* the voice of Spirit, and not just more subtle ego stuff?"

When you release all thought of what

your good is,
when you release all thought
that God is not to be trusted—
for what is resistance to Spirit but this belief?
and especially when you desire only to be empty,
then will you hear
the voice of the Holy One.

Marc,
I have come because you have called.
So it shall be for all the sons of God
held in the bondage of their own delusion,
yet who sense that salvation is possible.
No cry for deliverance is unheard by Me.

Now,
is it not but a small matter to recognize
your chosen purpose?
The result of such a choice you cannot see.
Nor is it your need to do so.
For when the soul chooses to serve God,
it serves mystery beyond reproach.
It is that which can be trusted completely.
For since the Son
first held the thought of Separation
has the Father sought to restore His place.
He alone knows the fruit of all service
given by the soul who sees beyond shadows.
I will share this with you
before ending this communication:
never shall I ask that you surrender
your own free will.
Yet,
you have asked to participate in the
awakening of the Son,
and so we have come to you.
Will you tarry yet awhile longer?

As you resist service to your brother

so, too, do you resist your own salvation.
These are one and the same.
I encourage you to follow your heart,
and place your trust not in the belief of the world,
but solely on the light of our Father
which is within you.
Herein lies what you long for.
Herein lies your final peace.
Here, I AM,
and I desire that all the sons of God
reside where I AM.

Indeed,
peace is but Love which longs
to share of itself,
and that is the light
which is come into the world.
It is time for the world to comprehend it.
What work could be grander than this?

What task of greater importance?
What, beloved brother,
can the world offer that can be remotely
as valuable to you?

"Seek first the Kingdom."
Marc, you have sought,
and you have found.

Now is the time for sharing,
that the world may comprehend Light,
and release darkness.

Fear not,
for I am with you always.
This you know well.
Live what you know.

Amen.

ↂ

That does it. Often during this experience with Jeshua, I have had the idea of scheduling a session with Jonah, who is the only person—perhaps I should say "entity"—whose authority I would trust. His guidance over the past three years has been uncannily accurate, and the profundity of his teaching unsurpassed. Whoever or whatever Jonah is, I have come to trust him completely. This doesn't mean I always follow his advice; in fact, quite the contrary. It seems that more often than not, if he suggests the high road, I take the low road. Following the low roads has eventually led me blundering into the humbling recognition that, in ways I do not yet understand, Jonah seems to see things from a much more inclusive vantage point than I.

Now there is no hesitation. I grab my writing pad, write out a list of questions, stuff it into an envelope, and hurriedly address it to Hossca Harrison, who serves as a channel for Jonah. I rush out into the blustery spring afternoon and run up to the corner mailbox. Just before dropping the letter into the mail slot, I silently ask Jonah to be perfectly frank with me in his answers.

Back in my apartment, I re-read the communication I just received. I thought I was past that fear of sharing this information. But it strikes me as so radical—it demands change at fundamental levels, and in ways I do not yet understand. How, then, can I share it?

ↂ

June 6, 1988

Now, we begin.

As you rest,
look out upon the beauty of your earth.
There is no lack of harmony there.
It is this sense of union
which attracts so many to nature.
Yet the question arises:
"Why do I not move in accord to this harmony?"
The 'I' to which I refer is mankind.

Marc,
I am in all things,
except in the perceptions of the world
so strongly adhered to by the mind of mankind.
In these things,
you will find Me not.

"Split wood, I am there.
Lift up a rock, there you shall find Me also."
It does not occur to the mind of one
so enchanted with illusion to consider
why I did not mention the marketplace,
or government!

The earth,
and all that abides in it,
knows no thoughts of Separation
from the Holy Father.
It is for this reason that all who desire to awaken
are attracted to nature.
It is why even I journeyed to the desert.

For when the noise of the world subsides,
the Kingdom may begin to be revealed.
That which facilitates silence
serves the awakening of the Son.

I wish to address your concerns over
The Jeshua Letters.
Seeing your doubt,
I offer this as prophecy.
Within two weeks,
you will receive your tape
from your beloved teacher, Jonah.
Here you will find
the confirmation you seek.

My question to you is this:
will you then create yet another defense

against the very purpose you have chosen?

Dwell upon this.

Amen.

Later, as I wash the dishes and stack them to dry, it suddenly occurs to me that Jeshua has given me something quite concrete! A prediction. One that has a clear message. If I do not hear from Jonah in two weeks, I will have fuel to discredit all of this! And now one question occurs: What if I *do* receive the tape?

∞

June 18, 1988

Turning off Tacoma Avenue, I drive down the hill, feasting my gaze on the harbor below. As always, a feeling of simple joy begins to settle in. I love living here, near the water yet above it, above the neighbor's rooftops, where I can see for miles, unobstructed by glass and concrete.

Pulling up to the old house whose top floor has become my home, I bound up the few steps to the front porch and flip open the lid of my mailbox. Immediately, I stop breathing, if just for a moment. There is a small package, a brown shipping envelope, just the right size for a cassette tape. A glance confirms it is from Hossca Harrison.

Walking much more slowly now, I go around the corner of the house, up the steps of the landing, and open the door that I forgot to lock when I left this morning. Once inside, my briefcase is gently tossed onto the sofa, the brown envelope on the dining room table, and I am in my rocker. Within seconds, my mind is full of avoidance thoughts: "I really need to get the laundry done, and it has been a long time since I vacuumed. Did I take the garbage out this morning?"

"Enough, already!" I shout out loud, and then more quietly, "Let's just get this over with."

I slip the cassette into the tape player and settle into my rocker. The harbor is so still tonight. There is only one tanker, waiting patiently to be pulled into the docks by those familiar green-and-white tugboats. The lights are beginning to shimmer across glassy waters, ribbons of dancing radiance disappearing into the hillside that lies just a block from me.

A clicking sound announces that the tape is ready, and I turn my attention to it, but leave my eyes on the soothing waters below.

"We have questions for Marc Hammer," says the recorded voice of Rebecca Harrison.

"So state it," booms the voice of Jonah. It is a voice so unique, so powerful, that it cannot be forgotten.

"Last year, I met with two friends at a cafe in Ballard..."

"Oh, quite by accident, say ye?" interrupts Jonah.

It has been my experience that he already knows the real intent of my questions before they are asked, as if replying to a deep level of genuine inquiry often inaccessible to my conscious mind.

He continues: "Is not all, my friend, that transpires, in accordance to one's beingness, by a grand design? Not a design by a force, or source, outside of oneself, but by a drawing of souls together to share with each other, to teach and to learn from each other, to bring back ancient memories that one forgets, because they are so shielded with the programmed consciousness."

"Indeed, as ye well know, and we have spoken to ye many times, your purpose—is it not?—is to bring forth an understanding of one's own inner enlightenment, one's own inner power, of assisting others through trauma. Indeed, of healing your own trauma..."

All of that from one seemingly innocuous question about a meeting with a few friends. He is already there, touching that space deep within me. I can feel it. It is not so much the words, but a feeling that is evoked. My ego, my protective mask, cannot shield me from this feeling.

And now, tears are flowing freely, as if my whole body is opening up.

The tears work their way—from cells in my legs, my arms, my chest, everywhere—up to, and out of, my eyes. I am a tingling, bawling mass of flesh. But it feels so good. The tears continue unabated throughout the remainder of the session, as I ask Jonah questions about my resistance, about my fear that it is all just an ego trip, about Jeshua...

"When one is preparing to change realities, to go from what would be termed as an old reality to that of a new reality, in the midst of that change the negative ego, the old, fearful programming, comes to the surface. Even that which would be termed as the hidden unconscious programming begins to surface.

"Ye have asked us in this energy to be blunt and frank with ye? Indeed, we will be."

He heard me! When I mailed the questions, I had silently asked Jonah not to hold any punches, to be frank with me. And is he ever!

"What are ye afraid of? What, indeed, in this life, is there to be afraid of? Death? What is death, but simply walking through one door to walk unto another door called 'birth.' It is the death of the old consciousness, the death of the old reality, to allow the birth of a new reality, a new dimension of life.

"Chance. What is this word 'chance'? An accident? Is the universe an accident? Is the earth an accident? Is the birth of a child an accident? Is the flight of a bird, the sound of a dolphin, the singing of a whale, or the birth of a star an accident? Is it all by chance? Or is it—indeed—a grand design of the Oneness of that termed 'God'? Never is there such called 'chance.' Ye were drawn to us because of your ancient memories of us. To break through the ego, that the heart might be found.

"Is it all by imagination? Indeed, my friend, one cannot imagine that which they have not experienced. Indeed, to ponder that statement. We well understand ye want a direct answer: 'yes' or 'no,' is this occurring? But it is to be perceived in this manner. Jeshua exists within everyone. To understand it in this manner, my friend, a part of ye *is* Jeshua. There is a part of that within each one. Jeshua is an energy, meaning 'Truth Giver.' Honor that which ye hear. Honor that which ye speak. What is of importance is to understand the symbology of this energy, meaning 'Truth Giver.'"

Suddenly and dramatically, everything which makes up the reality of this moment disappears. Simultaneously, I am electrified, every cell of my body alive as if charged by some unseen source of sublime energy, the energy of recognition.

There stands before me an image I now know well. It is the image of Jeshua, radiant in golden light, and about him—to the sides, below, and above—are other beings, equally as radiant. I somehow know they represent **all** beings who have ever lived, or ever will live. Their smiles and radiance express a joy that transcends all description. The person Jeshua, indeed, the whole of that lifetime **does** express the reality of Christ, **who is all of us**! My God, does his life make visible the truth of our very beings, mirroring back to our conscious minds what was so long ago forgotten? Was he, **is** he, the soul of each of us, whispering to our heart the only obvious truth?

Truth Giver. The tears have stopped. In fact, it feels as if everything has stopped, especially my mind. No grasping for bits and pieces to argue against. No resistance to what I feel, or what I experience. The words reverberate continually in my mind, resonating like an echo without end: "Truth Giver, Truth Giver, Truth Giver..."

⚬

July 19, 1988

Now, we begin.

Beloved brethren,
you who linger on the edge of Light
believing yet that darkness is your home,
allow Me to speak to you in this treasured moment,
which, by the way,
is not in time.

Time is the measure of illusion.
What is Real is always beyond time.

Again I would share with you,
that if you would penetrate
the veil of your experience
and find within it
that which can set you free,
you must go always to your feelings.
For the thoughts you hold are either
the products of other minds
held in the bondage of darkness,
or are born of your own insistence
on the truth of circumstance.

Never are you apart from the Kingdom,
save by your clearly free choice.
Contemplate this one truth deeply.
When you come to trust
the Father's will for you,
all doubt about your experience
will be forever banished.
Do not doubt this!

Yet I would share with you
that there are no roadmaps;
you are your path home.

It is thus that guidance is an art
requiring the greatest tenacity,
since you are constantly creating your experience.
My guidance is given
simply because you have asked for it.
Now, ponder this:
My life among you was nothing more
than your very own.
My experience of that time is wholly yours,
for the Son is indeed One.

See, then,
that Jeshua is not—
and was not—

apart from you,
but is a part of you.
It cannot be otherwise.

I give you no specific instruction
relative to the experience
you create, nor shall I.
It is not My purpose.
My purpose is to guide you on this,
the last part of your journey.
When you have come to where I AM,
it will be completed,
and a new one will emerge.
I will lead you
beyond all shadows
once,
and for always—
the shadows you know well.

This day,
remember that you are
the only begotten Son,
and that nothing matters save
the remembrance of Me.
Beyond all appearances,
this alone is the only experience
truly occurring for you,
as well as everyone.

This is preposterous
to the mind in bondage,
for remember always:
what appears as darkness is light
to the world,
yet that which is Light
is believed to be darkness.
There is no salvation in the perceptions of your world.
Therefore,
simply release them.

Soon, you will abide in Me wholly.
Herein lies the purpose of your
being in the world,
herein shall you know the intention of your soul.

Peace I give unto you,
My beloved brethren.

Amen.

⁌

July 21, 1988

Now, we begin.

Again, I come forth to you
for, again,
you have asked.

I AM That which resides
in the Heart of All.
I AM That which springs forth from the Father
and is before all worlds.
I AM That which has walked among you:
and the world knew Me not.
Beloved brethren,
peace I give unto you.

Not as the world can imagine,
give I forth unto you.
I call,
yet few hear.
Fewer still respond.

In all things,
rest first in Me,
and know your Father's will.
In all things,
heed not the teaching of the world,

*for what is born of ignorance
can lead only to ignorance.
But that which proceeds from Light
leads surely to Light,
for that Light,
it is.*

*Release all fear,
embrace all that you are,
and express in this the Light you are.
Not one hair of your head can be touched
when first you abide in Me.
Why fear a moment's fantasy?
For of such is the world made.
It means nothing.*

*Love alone is the substance
of all that is Real.*

*Go now,
in peace,
for I am with you always.*

Amen.

"I come forth to you for again you have asked." Re-reading the communication, my attention rests on that one line. I don't remember making any appointments with Jeshua! This isn't the only time he has spoken like that. Why? And why does it seem to matter to me? How could I ask, and not know I have done so?

I feel like Sherlock Holmes, trying to unlock the secrets of a mysterious occurrence. Sherlock picks up a paperweight and senses its importance, even though it remains beyond his understanding.

Like Sherlock, I put my own paperweight back down for now.

Chapter Seven

Not as the world gives,

give I unto you.

Yet my giving is but

your giving to yourself.

When will you choose to accept it?

August 17, 1988

"I just got a call from Wayne."

I put the last touches on the flow chart I've been designing; hit the F7 key to save the document, then turn in my chair to look at Geoff. "You what?"

"I just got a call from Wayne." Geoff is not smiling. In fact, a look bordering on pain is etched into his face. He glances at me, then at the floor. This does not feel good.

"What is going on these days back in Columbus?" I ask, referring to the headquarters of the software company that we work for. It has been a very satisfying relationship, and the future is bright.

Geoff turns his head away and looks out the window. Whatever it is, he certainly does not want to say it. "Wayne just told me that our paychecks might bounce."

"Come again?" I am sure I did not hear what I heard.

"He said our paychecks might bounce." Now Terry, our service technician, his ears perked by Geoff's words, bounds into my office with an inquisitive look of disbelief.

Geoff continues. "Damn! There are apparently some big problems with money right now. I don't know what is going on. Wayne may be the vice-president, but he doesn't seem to know much himself. *Something* is hitting the fan back there."

"What money problems?!" I interject. "We have done $150,000 in business the last two months, and they can't make salaries?"

Geoff winces. "I know, I know. Right now, I do not know what else to tell you. Damn!" His frustration explodes as he slams his fist into the wall, then takes a deep breath and sighs.

All three of us are on the phones to our banks, and the replies are the same. Our paychecks have bounced.

Frustration, anger, fear, confusion, and a sense of disorientation run rampant for the next several minutes. Finally we get through to Wayne, all three of us speaking at the same time from our individual office phones, until Wayne shouts for silence.

"Look! I am as much caught by this as you guys are. We *thought* we had $200,000 in backing from our financiers, and so we've been leveraging our assets to expand our markets, like yours out there in Washington. But it's been withdrawn. Maybe it wasn't there, I don't know. The bank has frozen our assets. There *is* no money available."

The reality is beginning to sink in. It occurs to me to ask about the commissions, especially the development fees due to us for the software products we had designed for the company. An amount of $10,000 is due to us in only 45 days.

After a long pause, Wayne speaks slowly. "It looks like *all* of it is history, Marc."

"What about the checks due in a week for the month of August?"

Silence is the only answer any of us needs to hear.

By the end of the day, it hits me full force. I have lost two months' salary, an additional few thousand in commissions, and—most significantly—my share of the development fees due on October 1st. *That* money is what I had joined this venture for. Even conservative royalty estimates had promised enough income to allow me to stop working every day in order to get to the next.

Then a paralyzing fear grips me. When all is said and done, I have enough funds to live through the month of October. And that's it.

I finally raise my eyes from my financial records and stare out the window at blackness, seeing only my own reflection blankly staring back. Much time passes this way, simply staring as if transfixed at—and through—this transparent image of myself.

Thoughts begin to whirl, chasing each other round and around, visions of what would have been, visions of what I had expected, visions of imagined disasters yet to befall me, all of them whirling around a central axis of Wayne's one message to us: "There is no money."

But now, something shifts. The image and racing thoughts dissolve, replaced by feelings, energy pulsating through me. I feel it first in my solar plexus, then building and pushing through my chest. I involuntarily begin to breathe very deeply, and the energy continues moving upward. Its quality is transformed as it seems to fill my head now, and suddenly I burst out laughing. God, I am laughing as I have not laughed in years, maybe never! It is not the laughter of nervousness, nor of helplessness. It is the laughter of freedom!

I haven't lost anything. No job has been lost, no royalties, no commissions—nothing. What has been lost is a weight, the weight of believing that I must strive to get ahead, to gain something I thought I did not have. No, nothing of any importance has been lost. The only thing that has happened is that a bubble has burst.

And as that realization sinks in, the phone rings.

∞

"Hello?"

"Hi, it's Kendra. I know this is probably going to sound weird, but is everything all right?"

Struck by the uncanny timing of her call, as well as her question, I do not answer immediately, and so she continues. "I was getting ready for bed, and suddenly I had this overwhelming urge to call you and, well, for a moment I was actually a little frightened. Pretty crazy, huh?"

What strikes me is that too few of us trust our intuition enough to act on it, as she has done. Sitting in the hard-backed chair next to the phone, I tell her all that happened today.

"God, that *is* scary! I don't know what I would do!" And, then, more softly, "What *are* you going to do?"

I pause, realizing I had not really thought about it, yet my answer comes quickly. "Well, I have my yoga classes which begin again soon. Maybe I'll expand them, maybe even get busy and do some promotional work. And, well, I am going to write."

The cat is out of the bag.

"Just what are you going to write?" Her voice betrays her suspicion that she already knows the answer.

"It feels like it is time to start... I mean, I am sitting here with no money to speak of, no idea what The Jeshua Letters is supposed to be. I feel like I am staring into a fog that obscures everything in front of me, yet I have the oddest feeling that the fog is utterly safe."

Kendra asks the obvious. "How are you going to make it?"

"That is the strangest part. At least, it seems strange to me. It seems so clear—at the moment—that all these years I have believed there is some sort of security out there in the world, and now it is like waking up from a dream or something. My rational mind wants to insist that this is just a momentary setback, and that I should start scrambling around again to create that security. But a deeper part of me seems to know there is no need, no purpose, in pursuing that course any more."

"Are you okay with that?"

I sigh, and Kendra is quiet, allowing me time to sort out my feelings. "Yes. Well, no. Well, I know it doesn't make sense, and yet in that moment when the bubble burst—it somehow made perfect sense. It feels, well, like it is what I am supposed to be doing. It is that deeper *feeling* that overrides my reasoning mind shouting thoughts of fear and panic."

Again, there is a long pause, as Kendra gives me room to continue my sorting.

"I don't know. Maybe I'm crazy. I guess the worst thing that can happen to me is that I'll end up a bag lady."

"A bag lady?"

"Yeah. I figure I'll have to wear a disguise so no one will see how embarrassed I am." We both laugh for a moment, then become silent again.

"Kendra, this is really affecting me. I mean, something is affecting me. This is not me, you know? I have no money to speak of, no job. I'm going through emotions over everything that happened so suddenly, like the rug just got swept out from under me. And yet beneath it all is this hidden, quiet sense of rightness. Like all of it is **all right.** Everything that happened, and everything that will happen."

"It confounds me, actually. Sometimes the rational voice within me becomes so loud that it seems to win me over, and I feel certain I am totally out to lunch, that I had better get my head back down into reality. But then that quiet, peaceful feeling re-emerges, and I feel very certain that what I am saying to you is what I am going to do. I am going to write the book."

Again, there is a pause.

"So," Kendra finally speaks, nearly at a whisper, "it's happening. I mean, it is actually **unfolding.**"

"Remember Castaneda's books?" I ask, knowing that they are among her favorites: "Remember when Carlos has to jump off the cliff into the black of night? Well, I feel like I have jumped without knowing I did so. Most of the time, it feels okay. But at other times I start kicking and screaming, even though I keep falling. And the falling feels absolutely right, no matter how strong my anxiety attacks are. It feels like it is happening in slow motion, yet I know that it is happening now, even as I speak with you."

Hearing my own words magnifies the reality of it all. I **have** jumped off the cliff, one I never thought I would consider going near. I am going to make **The Jeshua Letters** public, and let come what may.

"When do I get to read it?" Kendra asks.

My reply comes so quickly that the words seem to rumble out even before I can think them. "The manuscript will be done around Christmas, and I'll circulate a few copies among friends before I set about finding a way to publish it."

By Christmas?! I haven't even started transcribing the communications yet, nor do I have any idea what to do with them! Am I getting a taste of what it means to jump off the cliff?

"Kendra?"

"Yeah?"

"Mind if I share with you something really strange?"

She laughs, and her response to me is almost giddy.

"You mean all of this isn't strange enough?"

"Kendra, during the past few weeks, sometimes in meditation, sometimes just doing whatever, an image of a woman has appeared in my mind. With it, Jeshua has suggested that I go see this woman. At first, I was at a loss, yet I felt I **knew** her, even though it isn't someone I have ever met.

"Well, last week I suddenly remembered an old business associate who told me about a Christian mystic in Seattle he was quite fond of. It struck me deeply because he said that she 'speaks with Jesus.'

"Anyway, I got her name and number, and gave her office a call. I'm scheduled to meet with her tomorrow. When I made the appointment, I had no idea how I would be able to get away from work. Surprise, surprise!"

Our conversation ends with Kendra's unconditional support, together with her insistence that I tell her everything that happens when I meet with "that mystic lady."

❧

I am still fifteen minutes early, so I drive slowly by the stately old mansion—now named Gethsemane—which is both home and teaching center for Elizabeth Burrows. The box containing the communications is on the seat beside me, but it occurs to me not to show this to her. I do not so much want to talk about my experience as hear about hers. I'll just stay in the closet for now, thank you.

Turning around a few blocks away, I return and park the car, acknowledging my nervousness as I climb the steps and open the leaded glass door. Why am I here? "Just go with the flow, Marc, just go with the flow. *Trust,* remember?" I think to myself, trying to relax, to slow my breath.

Ms. Burrows' personal secretary greets me warmly and escorts me upstairs to the mystic lady's office. I hear her secretary announce me and, as she steps aside, I see Elizabeth standing up—all five feet four inches of her—face beaming in a large smile, hand extended warmly. We are already as old friends—at least, it feels like it to me.

Her hair is cropped short, and she is dressed completely in white. Apparently hearing my unasked question, she explains: "I choose to wear white, you see, as it is the clothing worn by the Essenes, of which I was one, at the time of the Master."

We fall easily into an intriguing conversation, talking about metaphysics, yoga, cosmic consciousness, her memories of life as an Essene, and her love for the Master, the one named Jesus. She is obviously very intelligent and well studied, and she speaks from personal experience about mystical states of awareness. In fact, she speaks of these things easily, as I might talk about the weather or a favorite restaurant.

"Elizabeth," I interject, "I recently had an experience I would like to ask you about."

Now I know why I left the communications in the box. I will not mention his name.

"I was sitting in meditation one day, when a being seemed to appear out of a field of golden light..."

I do not need to continue. A smile crosses her face; her eyes look not so much at me as *through* me, toward something, or someone who elicits a gentle joy, a love, a reverence, from her.

"That's Him."

"Him?" I ask.

"Oh, I mean 'He.'"

"No, I am certainly not correcting your English, but who is 'Him'?"

She looks directly at me, and says, "Why, the Master Jesus, of course," implying with her tone that I obviously knew it.

There is silence for a long moment, her eyes embracing me, and then she speaks. "I know now why you are here. There is something you are missing. Something He wants you to have. Please, follow me."

Like a dutiful and innocent child, I do so, following her down the stairway, my hand gently running along the top of the polished, wooden handrail. At the bottom of the stairs we turn and enter the library.

After looking through the bookshelves for a few moments, she picks out two volumes; one small and very thin, the other much larger and thicker. "Here we are," she says, handing them to me. "Our time together is now completed. I'll leave you to show yourself out."

Her departure catches me a bit by surprise, and after a moment I look down at books I have never seen before, even after twenty years of extensive study. The tiny book is entitled ***The Discovery of the Essene Gospel of Peace***, the larger one is a rendition of the ***Gospel of Peace*** written by Elizabeth. Electricity is running through my fingertips and up into my arms.

I know it is time to leave, and I do so, holding the volumes to my chest, which feels warmer and warmer. All the way back to Tacoma, there is an unmistakable feeling of joy. Occasionally I reach down, letting my hand rest on the books, caressing them, smiling.

EVERYTHING IS AS IT SHOULD BE. TRUST.

Back in my apartment, I sit down in the living room, bathed in serene afternoon sunlight filtering through the blinds, books on my lap. Again, I run my hands over them, pulse quickening. She was right. These are what I was sent for. I know it without even reading them!

Not hurrying, savoring this experience of clarity, I open the larger book, and as I read, tears begin to come—tears of joy, tears of recognition. Beyond even the slightest trace of doubt, I know I am reading the teachings of the Master, of Jesus, of Jeshua.

A tremendous burst of energy moves rapidly up my spine, exploding in a flood of images, scenes, memories of another life—a life that is surely mine. As the images flow through me, felt in every cell, my tears flow freely, releasing a deep tension that has unwittingly held back the memories. The tears simultaneously seem to flood me, nurture me, and bathe me in a joy beyond words.

For a moment, I see with my mind's eye the face of Jonah, and recognize the identity of the "Great One." My teacher, my friend, my guru: Jeshua, the one called Jesus.

∞

September 4, 1988

Now, we begin.

Again,
you have chosen to prepare a place for Me,
and so I come now unto you.

Beloved,
· *is it not without effort that*
the Kingdom is entered?

What struggle must be experienced,
what obstacle overcome?
Is not such perception founded on the belief
that illusion is Reality?

Never are you separate
from your Holy Father.
You simply choose to insist that you are.
Herein is the birth
and continuance
of all struggle,
all fear,
all doubt.
Penetrate this truth wholly,
and illusion will be no more.
Shall we tarry longer?

The Father awaits
the return of the Son,
with patience born
of incomprehensible love.

There are no wrong turns in your journey,
nor in anyone's.
You know this is madness to the world,
but the world is madness.
Release it.

This day I shall speak only briefly,
for what needs to be shared is simple.
I await you just beyond the edge
of your resistance to a purpose
freely given,
and accepted.
I AM the end of your pain,
which the journey of Separation is.
You are but a breath away now,
yet your resistance is your path
to the abode of the Father.

Embrace every moment of your experience wholly.
Celebrate it.
This will quicken the process
of final release.

The Jeshua Letters is the beginning
of our work together;
your purpose is to allow it
into the fabric of illusion
which traps the Father's Son.
It is the creation of another door
leading from illusion to Reality.

Enlightenment is inevitable.
Remember this always
as you gaze upon your fellow dreamers.
Serving the Atonement
is to know the effortless joy
of the Father's will.
All else is but resistance to this.

I am always here,
and will participate with you
in this most joyous work
of atoning the momentary imagination
of Separation
whenever you choose to recognize Me,
instead of the world.

Peace unto you.

Amen.

September 7, 1988

Now, we begin.

Beloved brethren,

I would ask that you pause
in the movement of your dream,
that I might share with you this moment.

I am not lost to you,
and I assure you that
you are not lost to Me.
"Lift up a rock, and there
you shall find Me also."
How long will you choose to wait
for what is necessarily inevitable?
The Dreamer will, indeed, awaken.

To see with new eyes
is to transform the world,
which is entirely of your making,
from a world of darkness
into a world of Light.

To see with new eyes
requires only that you abandon
those perceptions which already
you know cannot work.
The Kingdom you seek
cannot be found where you are.
It is, however,
where I AM.
The distance between us is never
more than this simple choice:
to release your insane insistence
on separation from your Holy Father.

I am Jeshua.
I am available to you whenever
you decide to choose
to know Me.
There is not the least difficulty in this,
for it is simply to choose
to truly be who you already are,

and have forgotten.
As you come to know Me,
the recognition will dawn that what I AM
exists everywhere
as the substance of all things.

As you come to know Me,
the recognition will dawn
that you are already all
that I represent
to the consciousness of humanity.
As you come to know Me,
the recognition will dawn that
there is no distance to travel,
no growth to occur, no error to correct,
save one:
your insane perception of yourself
as separate from Me.

You are as a rich man
who travels forth with a purse
of jewels and gold coins,
searching constantly for the treasure
he is certain is there for him,
forgetting the purse clutched
tightly in his hands.

Consider this image,
and allow it to transform your perception,
for this is a very accurate image
of what you have chosen to be.
You are entirely free to make your choice anew.

Remember always that the
truth of the Kingdom is utterly beyond
the capacity of your world.

Therefore,
seek not guidance from the world,

for it cannot lead you
to what lies beyond the world:
the Kingdom,
and the treasure you seek
in all your longings.
I am with you always,
though rarely do you recognize Me.
I am the very heart of what you are,
always,
though you struggle to deny it.

When you release your Dream—
which is wholly insane—
the Reality of who you are
will alone remain.

Herein lies the end
of your travel.
Herein lies peace.
Herein, I AM.
Come home to Me.
Come home to your true Self,
and celebrate with Me this one fact:
"I and My Father are One."

Peace be unto you,
My beloved brethren.
Not as the world gives,
give I unto you.
Yet My giving is but
your giving to yourself.

When will you choose to accept it?

Amen.

October 4, 1988

Now, we begin.

It is not without much hesitation
that I come forth unto you
at this time.
This hesitation occurs because
there is again a resistance building within you,
though at very subtle levels.

During this pivotal transformation
you are moving closer than ever before
to dissolution in Me.
It is a time of critical importance,
for the ego—
the habit of separation—
will rise yet more steadfastly
to block this from occurring.
To the conscious mind it appears
that all is well,
but at very refined,
very deep levels,
I assure you that it is not.

Therefore,
I hesitated to come forth,
for it was possible that the resistance
would again be your habitual choice,
thus rebuilding the wall we have
worked so diligently to dismantle.

I am pleased that—
in a very critical moment of this contact—
you chose in your soul to open to Me.
It was at this point that
the clear vision of Light appeared to you,
and you beheld various images
granting recognition of My presence.

You are very much like a warrior
engaged in your last battle.
The "enemies" take on subtler form,
and can therefore go unnoticed.
It was I who spoke to you this morning,
suggesting you arise.
It is a great truth that receptivity to guidance
is most present during the time
of the early morning.
A touch of sleepiness,
I might add,
enhances the receptivity.

Come into the mountains tomorrow.
Do not allow the "shoulds"
of your illusion to take precedence.
The emotions you have been feeling—
beginning last evening
are the result of your denial of Me.
This you well know.

You have chosen to participate
in the bringing forth
of a knowledge so sublime,
so simple,
as to seem ungraspable.
It is the knowledge of living in Christ wholly.

Again,
I reiterate that this
is a crucial time for you.
Let not your path be shaken.
All the universe moves to support you at this time,
as it does whenever—
and wherever—
a soul stands on the brink
of fully awakening.

Do not allow your habit—

born of Separation—
force yet another denial of this support.
To the degree you allow support,
support is given.
This is the bounty of your Father's table.

This communication brings forth no new teaching.
What has been given forth as The Jeshua Letters
is now finished.
The completion of this project is inevitable now.
Following this shall come
specific guidance from us,
and I shall continue to refine this Teaching as required,
for the benefit of the many levels
of human consciousness.

Tomorrow,
when you journey to your mountains,
you will establish contact
with an entity—
a soul—
who will begin to give forth to you
the wisdom of the earth,
which you have asked for.

Marc,
I well perceive your incredulity.
"God, another one!?" you think to yourself.
Is it not time to simply
be what you have chosen:
a messenger of the heart,
opening, receiving, and sharing
the wisdom of perfect knowledge
to assist in the awakening of man?

This is not a grand thing,
but the simplest of the simple:
the inevitable conclusion to the drama
of Separation,

for Light cannot be ultimately denied.

Soon now,
the consciousness of man
will bask in the glory of the Son's remembrance

Rejoice,
and allow your return to Light
to be fulfilled.

Amen.

I manage to get to Kendra's just as she is pulling out of her driveway for the one-hour ritual drive to work.

"Take a moment and read this, will you?" I hand her the communication, and, for a moment, she looks at me with an unspoken question in her eyes. She probably isn't used to having people pull into her driveway at 7:30 in the morning insisting that she stop to read things like this. She shivers suddenly. As she finishes reading, she hands it back to me, and I detect a trace of tears in her eyes.

"It's finished," she says with quiet resolution. "You know, I didn't shiver because I'm cold."

"I know."

She turns and walks back to her car, slides in, closes the door, and rolls the window down. "So, what are you going to do now?"

"Well, it seems I am in quite a spot, aren't I?"

Her face is quizzical. "What do you mean?"

"Kendra, the only way I will ever know if any of this is valid is to do it, all of it. Not just write the book, but strive to live it. Only, what Jeshua talks about doesn't seem to be the kind of thing one can learn to do. It seems you either choose to be it, or you don't."

She nods her head, looking at the dashboard. "I know. I think, sometimes, we **all** know it." Lifting her head, she gazes out through the windshield, her eyes focused on nothing in particular.

"Yes, I think we all know it. But living it seems to be another matter."

Now she looks back at me. "I suppose I better get on to work, or is it back to my dream? So, what are you up to for the rest of the day?"

It had been my intention to spend the day looking for work. I guess my rational side had been winning the battle. I shrug my shoulders and smile. "I'm going to the mountains."

Chapter Eight

When you release your dream

—which is wholly insane—

the Reality of who you are

will alone remain.

December 16, 1988

There have been times during the past several months when I have felt very clear about not only this book, but about Jeshua. During those times, I cannot help but give thanks; rather than commuting on congested highways, my time is spent enjoying the peace and quiet of my home, allowing the manuscript to take shape around the communications from Jeshua.

But there are other times—of anxiety, of questioning, of doubt—and I am convinced that surely this must be crazy. Well, almost convinced.

Always, when the tirade of self-criticism abates, there comes a quiet voice speaking to me, heard only when I choose stillness within. He is there, always, assuring me that all is as it needs to be, reminding me that my task is to trust.

Last week, during one of my anxiety attacks about small details like paying the rent and buying food, I put the thought out to the universe that I just can't do this, that I am, after all, not very good at jumping off cliffs! Isn't there a nice, comfortable job out there? The very next morning the phone rang, and I answered it to receive an offer for just that! My first impulse—probably out of habit—was to grab it fast, before the lifeline was withdrawn. But something made me stop. I made an excuse about needing time to think about it.

I tried to spend the day just tinkering around the apartment, but grew restless and took a long walk. It is not often that December provides such a pleasant and dry opportunity in the Northwest. I ended up on a bench at a deserted pier along Ruston Way, watching a sea otter lazily playing in the water twenty yards away.

I feel caught between two worlds, knowing that I am unable, or unwilling, to return to the old world, yet only faintly recognizing the one ahead. It is a world without familiar roadmaps and signposts, a world which I am hesitant to enter. But behind my internal, intellectual hair-pulling is a feeling, a sense that somehow, in some way, I am going to emerge there, where He is, wherever that is, and in spite of myself.

I know well now, after this year and a half with Jeshua, what is required of me, *if* I truly want to be in what He calls the "Kingdom." It means giving up all the familiar ways I have cultivated for dealing with life, or what I *thought* was life. Whether those ways are effective or not is beside the point. It means releasing the unconscious belief that my life is *mine*, in the common view we all have of "me." Habits are not easily broken, or is it that "I" *can't* break it, since "I" a*m*, fundamentally, the habit?

As I watched the sea otter comfortably swimming about just off the end of the pier, I began to think that maybe those crazy physicists working on the cutting edge of quantum theory are close to the truth, closer than perhaps they realize. Or are they masters come to us in disguise to prod us out of the structures of our thoughts, the shadows on our cave walls? They speak of an odd reality, in which all possibilities are somehow already present, hidden in some invisible bag of eternity, waiting—waiting for us to do but one thing: to make a choice as to which "reality" we will manifest. We are the ones with the power after all, always.

According to Jeshua, those "infinite possibilities" come wrapped in two packages: one is labeled the "Kingdom," and the other, "Dream." The Dream holds within it a seemingly infinite number of possibilities: all the worlds and lifetimes lived before us, lived after us, lived now as us. All of these worlds are founded on one cornerstone: Separation, inseparably united with one fundamental energy, the energy of fear. Collectively, we believe so strongly in it that it goes unquestioned. We live in separation from each other, from nature, from God. Because we insist on being separate, we choose without hesitation the package labeled "Dream," and immediately find ourselves right here, right now, in a world we have believed to be real and independent of us. Or is it but a mirror reflecting nothing but our choice?

"Maybe," I thought to myself, "maybe the world keeps revolving round as it does, wars and greed and the like, because we insist it is real, and then struggle to find ways to deal with it. Have we given the package labeled 'Dream' our power? Have we given the very power of the Son away to our illusions?"

In Tibetan Buddhist metaphysics, it is said that at death the soul leaves the body and begins ascending to the clear light of the Dharmakaya, the "Body of Truth." However, faced with the overwhelming power and beauty of this light, the soul—habitually identified with its sense of being a separate self—recoils out of fear. This recoil creates a heaviness, and the soul sinks down, eventually back into yet another round of birth and death in a physical body, and all because the soul misunderstands its own nature, insisting on being separate!

Perhaps the packages aren't offered only once. Perhaps they are offered to us every morning as we wake up, or every moment, for that matter. Is the Light always available, and the death we fear but a moment's delusion?

Perhaps if we all decide to choose anew, right here wherever we are, right now whatever we are, the world we will manifest will be different, so very different. Different because we will seek not to create our world, but the world intended by a mystery forever beyond us, yet a mystery that resides right in our very core, at the center of our own truest selves.

The sea otter disappeared beneath the surface of the bay, swimming off to explore and play in other worlds. I waited for a moment, hoping he would surface again, then turned and walked home.

Back in my apartment, I stared at my computer, unable to find anything to say, not sure what the direction of this book is to be. It is still ahead of me, somewhere in that fog, the one without any signposts.

I spent the evening watching television, that great god of culture forever reassuring us of what is real. Finally, I pointed the remote control at the picture of some newscaster—they all look and sound the same, don't they?—and zap! The world disappeared!

It seems so clear, so simple! And yet a trace of something inside me is still resisting. Separation, and all that comes with it—where is the button, and how do I push it? How do I change channels? How do I finally and irrevocably release the package labeled "Dream"? Am I sure I want to?

⌒∞⌒

Marc, arise and write, please.

The voice startles me, and my eyes pop open.

"Ohhh, damn." I lift my head with a struggle and turn to look at the clock. It is 11:30, and I feel very tired.

"Can't we do this in the morning?" I ask my unseen visitor, then chuckle to myself at the nonchalance with which this conversation is taking place.

Yes.

God, I love the feeling of His presence so much, and think how nice it would be to just curl up on His "lap" and sleep forever.

At three o'clock, you will be awakened, and we shall continue.

Three o'clock! I was thinking more along the lines of nine o'clock, or even later. I feel his energy subside, and quickly fall back asleep.

Out of a myriad of cascading thoughts and images, awareness emerges. I realize I am awake.

"Damn, damn, double damn!" I sink down in the covers. It is so nice and warm here, and so cold out there! I know, I'll just ignore this. Giving it everything I can, I toss restlessly for awhile.

Suddenly, my eyes pop wide open. Looking out of the corner of my eyes, I see the clock clearly. It is 3:34, and I have to go to the bathroom. No warning at all, I just have to go to the bathroom, and it won't wait another minute.

Disgustedly, I throw the covers back and grab my robe. On the way to the bathroom I lift my eyes upward, muttering under my breath, "Boy, you guys will stop at nothing, will you?"

Now we begin.

You are losing the battle, Marc.
Losing,
but loss is not our aim now.
Soon,
there comes a clear sign unto you
of the work in which you participate,
the work of the Son's atonement.

When you clearly choose
the active participation in this work,
there will be nothing
which will not be provided.

There is no need to return
to your former dreams,
and is this thought
not the reason for your apparent misery?

Now is the time
of your final choice upon you.
The choice is but
between Love, and fear.
Fear is your habit,
the Dream of humanity,
and the denial
of the Son's rightful inheritance.

It is an inheritance,
the acceptance of which,
is a choice which must be made alone,
only because it was once alone denied.

There is no effort
experienced in the Kingdom.
There is only the manifestation

of the Father's will for you
and through you—
a demonstration that touches
the sleeping soul of the Son
cloaked momentarily in a dream of aloneness,
stumbling through fields
strewn with the corpses of death,
and that which is even now dying.
For Separation from the Father
is death,
and nothing more.

When you choose
the abundance of the Kingdom,
there is born a way of living
which requires no planning,
no achievement,
no securing of one's survival.
All is prepared before you,
the one who serves first
the Father who is within you.

Awakening from the Dream
seems painful
only to the degree
that one resists arising from
the temptation of illusory sleep,
and the apparent need of it.
This sleep is but the habit,
cultivated since the choice was made,
to inhere in the Dream of Separation.

Would you not choose with Me
the Reality of the Kingdom?
In it is all you can ever imagine,
every need fulfilled
before even a single request is made.
For surely your Father knows
you have need of these things.

You have experienced
the many aspects of Separation.
This world you know well.
Has its allure
not clearly failed you?
Choose, then,
only to release your
useless dream,
and be born again
into the experience of the Kingdom.
This choice gives birth
to a process of recognition
that quickly re-establishes remembrance
of the Son's rightful place.
For you will sit
at the right hand of the Father,
reviewing naught
but the splendor of a magnificence
unimaginable within the paltry,
and painful,
Dream of Separation.

The dream of fear,
which is all of mankind's worlds,
contains not a trace
of true joy,
only of apparent pleasures
lasting but an instant.

Choose, therefore,
That which is everlasting.
Choose therefore
That which abides forever,
and whose boundaries
are never reached.
Choose, therefore,
the presence of the Father
within you,

and the Kingdom
is all you will experience around you.

What life could be lighter
than one requiring
not a trace of struggle?
What joy could surpass participation
in the eternal abundance
which is the presence of the Father,
and the awakening of the Son,
in everyone
living the dreadful Dream
you have for so long suffered?

We love you greatly.
Yet we cannot choose for you.
We merely guide you,
pointing the way
only when asked,
patiently awaiting recognition
of the Dream
to dawn in the consciousness
of a mind habituated to shadows,
a recognition
of the Dream's depravity.

Choose the Kingdom wholly,
and the Dream shall be no more.
It vanishes from the mind forever,
leaving only incredible peace,
and wonder that the Dream
could have ever been dreamt.

There is no lack in the Kingdom.

Your only task—
if we may call it that—
is to experience in joy
the absolute safety and abundance

of the Father's table.

This simple choice
demonstrates a truth,
buried deeply in the heart
of every son yet sleeping.
To witness this choice
is the act of being nudged into waking,
until all the sons of man
are again living as
the Truth they are:
the one Son,
begotten of the Father
before all worlds,
partaking in the abundance
freely given,
the presence of the Father.

Herein lies
the Kingdom
of heaven on earth.
Can there be,
in truth,
any choice but this?

For a moment, I pause. The energy which is Jeshua has suddenly abated, and I find myself gazing at the flickering lights on the black and quiet waters of the harbor. There is the faintest of feelings within me, a pulsing of some sort. Surrendering my resistance, I breathe deeply and slowly, allowing abdomen, ribs, and chest to expand and release without strain.

While the intensity of this pulsing, this vibration, does not grow, it seems to expand in all directions, and then becomes softer and softer, drawing me more deeply into it. Though my eyes are open, I catch a glimpse of colored lights, felt as much as perceived.

Images begin flashing on the screen of my awareness at incredible speeds. I embrace the emotion each brings, recognition dawning that each is a part of me, each a lifetime, stretching back further and further, seemingly without beginning. They appear and disappear in an instant. As they fall away, I feel my body melting within itself, a deepening peace embracing, penetrating every cell. I am dissolving, letting go of all traces of resistance, all traces of denial, all traces of doubt—dissolving more and more completely. Increasing space now between the images as they become fewer, and fewer, and fewer until...there are none.

I do not know how much time goes by, for here, time is not.

From the silence of an emptiness which is forever perfect fullness, there emerges awareness, first of the reflection of my face in the window before me, then of the ships at rest in the harbor, the still waters, the flickering and radiant lights. They all seem to be contained within the reflection on the window, they in me and I in them; I am one with all things. In my reflection a faint smile begins to grow, a smile that springs gently from the center of my heart.

I did not know it would be like this. I would never have guessed it. Sitting here in this wonderful old rocking chair, the world so quiet in this pre-dawn hour, nothing special taking place. Everything the same, yet everything so different!

For this moment of eternity, gone the Dream.

Tomorrow I will start writing.

>*Now,*
>*it is finished.*
>*Already,*
>*the choice is made.*
>
>*Now,*
>*the recognition*
>*is completed,*
>*coming as a thief in the night,*
>*stealing the cobwebs*
>*of shadows,*
>*revealing the illusion*

of a long-standing Dream
to the Son who remembers.

The end of a lonely journey,
and the celebration
of one begun anew.
It is not a journey to,
but within,
the Kingdom.
Thus is My promise fulfilled,
for the Dream is burnt forever
in the glory of the Father's presence.

Now,
does life begin anew.
Now,
does life fulfill itself.
And this,
without effort.
Welcome home,
beloved brother,
welcome home.

Amen.

Chapter Nine

There is no effort in the Kingdom.

February 10, 1989

"There. It's finished." I mutter under my breath, as I save the draft for *The Jeshua Letters* in a file, some part of me hopes it disappears into the strange black hole of cyberspace, that cosmic junkyard where the Gods of Computerland eat up everything not backed up or printed out! If this book could be so eaten, just maybe that part of me could rest as it gradually resumed authority and control over my life.

I am startled at the chuckle that comes as the thought ends. It surprises me because it has emerged from a place much deeper than where my ego lives, as though I just discovered a room in my house I didn't know even existed.

As I push back from my keyboard, I notice for the first time that it is dark, and a glance at the clock reveals it is eleven pm. I realize I've been living in a very different world for the last seven weeks. I even missed Christmas, though I must say I can't even remember thinking about it!

The writing has meant a deep immersion in all that Jeshua has shared with me, and I have been occasionally surprised when a strong feeling would come over me leading to the removal of copious amounts of material. At times I have heard Him say, "not yet." Was it the personal information about His life? The controversial matter of the 'End Times'? The visions He has shown me about what this Work is to be in the future?

There is no rational explanation for this, only a deep inner sense of rightness, and I trust that completely…I think!

Some things He has said recently keep stirring within me:

> *Choose then, only to release your useless dream, and*
> *be born again into the experience of the Kingdom.*

> *This choice gives birth to a process of recognition that quickly re-establishes remembrance of the Son's rightful place.*

That shoots a hole in what I now see has been the entire thrust of my 'spiritual path' since 1973, when I took up meditation and yoga, along with study of the world's religions and psychologies. I see now, with extraordinary clarity, that all of it was based on a 'me' striving to attain, to gain a knowledge and (I humbly admit) a control over my life. Now it all appears in this new light as simply a dream, based on a false premise: I have looked the enemy in the face and seen it is but a 'me' that is little more than a habit cultivated since the choice was made to exist in the Dream of Separation!

After all these years, I feel like I have only truly just begun. What is it He alludes to as this mysterious 'process of recognition'? Do I get to peek around the corner to see if it is safe?

Now, that thought brings an outright laugh; what a hoot! Who could be asking such questions if not that smaller part of me that is the habit of separation—rooted in fear—I once fully identified as my self?

How can I ever hope to discover what this mystery means, unless I fully submit to the way of love Jeshua reveals, and to which he has called us?

⌘

I rise from my chair, and shake off the stiffness in my legs as I roam to the kitchen for a cup of tea. While the water races to boiling, I break off mint leaves and breathe in their scent. I drop the leaves into the pot, and watch them as they are rolled and tossed in the water. A part of me senses that I am not unlike those mint leaves, plopped into waters I had heretofore been ignorant existed, while claiming all sorts of 'knowledge' about those very waters.

I feel embarrassed. I feel reduced to being not unlike a marriage counselor who has never been married, or a UFO expert who has never seen one...ugh!

Returning to my desk, I realize I was wrong. It's not finished, yet. This manuscript isn't finished, and I most certainly am not. I can feel it: this old nemesis that has lived so long and so deeply within me. This nemesis emerging from within the shadows of my own existence so clearly I am startled—no, shocked—that I could have looked past it in avoidance for so long. This nemesis has a name, and it is 'Fear.' I don't mean the kind of fear I felt in Vietnam, or at plenty of other moments. This is something else, something deeper. Something in the fabric of my very soul, if that makes any sense.

My body shudders suddenly. For it is clear to me that the only way to be free of this nemesis will somehow require that I be lived into Reality. What's more, radically so, is that this is actually God 'taking the final step for me'! Whoa! Where is there hope for any modicum of control in that?! Yet, He promises the result will be to arrive in a new land, a land that is the opposite of fear: Love.

Love. Sweet, sweet love! I thought I knew something about it, but now as I sip this delicious mint tea and hear the nearly freezing rain begin to pelt my window, I must accept I have known little—if anything—of its true nature. The love Jeshua speaks of certainly cannot have anything to do with what I deem pleases me, since that 'me' has been steeped in the soup of ego. I feel reduced, yet again, to being a mere child, a child with much to learn.

And what about His cryptic statement:

> *Soon, there comes a clear sign unto you of the Work*
> *in which you participate, the Work of the Son's*
> *atonement. When you clearly choose the active*
> *participation in this Work, there will be nothing*
> *which will not be provided.*

A clear sign! Yahoo! I could use some of those! Or, again, are they needed only by that now smaller part of me so used to fearful apprehension often hidden behind a smile?

I pull up the file again and find myself drawn to words I know I feel a deep resistance to:

> *There is no effort experienced in the Kingdom. There*
> *is only a manifestation of the Father's will through*
> *you; a demonstration that touches the sleeping Son*
> *cloaked momentarily in a dream of aloneness.*

I flip through the printed pages of His recent communications, my
eyes stopping on one more strange statement:

> *The completion of this project is inevitable now.*

"Right!" I suddenly shout. "What the hell do I know about writing
a book, much less getting it published! And who the f--- would
read this crap anyway, and why would they want to? Now, this thing
actually becoming a book people read. Now, that would be a 'clear
sign,' ha!"

Really, I am screaming these thoughts, as though attempting to rebuff
some unseen advancing army trying to storm my castle! My body
shudders again. Not once, but twice. Three times, actually. What the
heck is He talking about? That nemesis I thought I had buried deep
enough to be rid of—like a cancer under control—is suddenly and
literally kicking and screaming:

"No! Not me! I'm not worthy! Look at me! Look at my utter failures!
I mean, I'm really the worst of the worse! There's nothing that could
be possibly manifest through me of any value at all, nothing!"

That final word explodes from the realm of thought, and a body
shaking and trembling, into a loud, defiant scream that shakes me to
the core.

I give up fighting it, all of it. If 'allowing' is the key to the Kingdom,
then I may as well start with this sudden gushing of tears from a well
deep within my heart and belly. The strength goes from my legs, and
I collapse onto the floor. The tears—interspersed with a litany of self-
loathing arguments—increase their flow. Yet the floor is comforting
somehow. I surrender into this darkness, rather than fighting it. And
touch for a moment, even as the flow continues, a hint of peace, of
real peace.

The early morning clanging of garbage cans wakens me. I don't know when I fell asleep, or whether the tears stopped before sleep, or because of it. Rising, I peer out of the icy windows to watch the garbage collectors do their important—and underrated—job.

What would they do if this was happening to them? What would anyone do? All of a sudden, an idea crashes head first into my whole being:

"I'm getting out of this cold, dark, dreary place. I'm gonna go to Hawaii again!"

Energy is surging through me as I pull out my suitcase from the closet.

"What, Marc, no careful planning?" My, things are changing!

The thought occurs to me to print out the draft of **The Jeshua Letters**. I see myself, as though in a movie, delivering it to Kendra on the way to the airport.

A week later, I am walking up the steps to her door, manuscript tucked under my arm.

Chapter Ten

When the soul chooses to serve God,

it serves mystery beyond reproach.

It is that which can be trusted completely.

February 17, 1989

The fire blazes before me as Kendra sits down on the couch, handing me a cup of hot spiced wine.

"A bit early for a touch of vino, don't you think?"

"You know me! It's Saturday, and it's never too early to enjoy my day off. Besides, not all of us have the freedom to traipse off to Hawaii!"

I make no response. I just look into her eyes. I remember thinking exactly that way. Was it just a short time ago? Did I really believe I was not free to follow the depth of my heart, and that 'reality' was *out there,* in a job I didn't really love? Of course I did. In this internal tug-of-war, a part of me clearly still believes I, too, should 'get back down to earth,' except that an emerging larger part of me—a part I am only beginning to know—simply won't succumb to that anymore.

Kendra seems to be knowing exactly what I am thinking.

"I guess I am still using my freedom to insist on this habit of living I am so familiar with!" She smiles weakly, and sips her hot spiced wine.

Glancing at the manuscript in its light blue cover, she looks at me. "Is that what I think it is?"

"Yes. It doesn't feel like it's done yet, but yes, that's it. I thought you could, you know, read it through for me, while I'm gone."

Her hands rests on it, but she suddenly changes her mood, and mind.

"So, you never told me what happened on your winter excursion into the mountains."

I was really hoping she wouldn't ask. It has been a month since that trip, yet her question evokes effortlessly a renewal of the impact that day has had; I wonder if it will ever really move from the present into the category of 'history.' My hand shakes a bit as I put down my hurriedly emptied cup, and move to stand nearer the fire. There are parts of that journey I don't want to share. Things that disturbed me. I elect to take a well trodden path.

"First, the good news! I found my way to a stream, and brushed the snow off a large rock, sat down, and waited."

"What happened?" she asks.

"Nothing. Well, for sometime, nothing, that is. Except that I fell into this delightful rhythm. It seemed like my breathing naturally found its way into resonance with the sound of the water flowing over nearby rocks."

I move back to sit facing her on the sofa, and take her hands in mine impulsively.

"That's when I heard her."

"Her? You mean Jeshua, don't you?"

"No, her! Definitely female."

"Who?"

"M... " I stop. "Don't even think of asking," I reply with a quiet firmness.

Kendra looks hard at me, nods her head 'okay,' while her hands are squeezing mine a bit tighter, as if to encourage me to continue. Her willingness to respect my boundary somehow allows me to do so.

"I would swear I could hear her, feel her presence, and—at least in my mind—see her, as plainly as I am seeing you right now.

"She did something. It felt as though she touched the top of my head. All this energy started to sort of swoosh around and around. I felt dizzy, but blissfully so.

"Then, she spread her arms out, and as she did, I felt like some subtle

175

part of me, more fluid than this body, expanded with her.

"Then, effortlessly, Kendra, I could feel the trees, the snow, the rocks, the water! And I mean, feel them from the inside out. Feel them like I never have before! Maybe, in fact, for the truly first time!

"At some point, I remember her saying to me, 'Now, you know your true body. It is this precious earth herself that gives you entrance to this realm. Love her as you learn to love yourself.'

"Kendra! Stop! You are going to break my fingers!" I shout.

"Oh! So sorry!"

I can feel the blood rushing back, skin beneath fingernails becoming pink again.

"That is so beautiful!" Kendra's eyes are watering, and I sense her whole being open and soften, but my response doesn't match hers. Noticing, she grabs my chin the way my mother used to when she demanded some hidden secret from me.

"Come on! What else."

"Kendra, I'd rather not talk about it. I mean, I don't know if I can."

Maybe it's time to go back to the fire. Rising, I step to it, and gaze into its flames for a moment.

"She showed me the future."

"She what?!"

"She showed me the future. Kendra, I saw twisted heaps of concrete rubble, and, and people huddled around fires in deserted streets, and..."

"Wait a minute! You saw these things?"

"Yes! All like a high speed movie right where the trees had been! It scared me, and suddenly it all stopped, and the trees were there again, just as they had been. Only, well, I could not feel them as I had done a few moments prior.

"That is when I felt her soften. She told me there is not much time left, time to correct the spell mankind has fallen under, a spell in which we have forgotten that the earth is really our true body, that we are all one family and...and..."

"And, what? Don't you dare stop now!"

"That in reality there is only one of us here! One being, one soul, caught in a spell, a dream. There is only one of us here!"

"But, isn't that what Jeshua has said to you, too? 'You never look upon another, for you see only your self?'"

"Well, yes! But, that makes no sense! Damn, Kendra! And this future junk! I don't like this stuff! It makes my skin crawl, just as when Jeshua has shown me similar things."

"What!? When did He do that? Are you hiding things from me?"

I've been caught in my own admission, for sure.

"Hey! I plead the fifth amendment on the grounds it may later incriminate me!"

By the look on her face, that ploy isn't going to cut it with her.

"Y-yes, yes He has. And more. Much more, but He has said it is not yet time for all that. He has spoken of a time coming when America will feel very safe and comfortable, and then that will be shattered. But we will still think the ego's way of thinking can save the day."

I need to sit down again. I speak softly.

"But it won't happen. Only then will we, will the whole world, begin to realize government, or big business, nothing can keep things the way they have been. That we will be forced by the failure of our own miscreations to undergo a massive shift of consciousness. He said that with each passing day, while not being fated, the images shown me are becoming an increasing probability.

"But He also stressed that even what may come soon will become part of the awakening, the 'end times' the Bible talks about, except that they have been seriously misconstrued. It's not a punishment, because God does not punish. We create our experience, and we are all so inextricably linked that, well, that there is really only one of us, one soul that is Humanity, and in it the fullness of Christ already resides, stirring to be remembered, rising to be the authority from which we create, rather than fear and the ego it generates.

"He calls it the 'Adamic Process.'" Kendra is about to ask the same question I asked Him, so I beat her to the punchline.

"He said He will be revealing more about that in the proper time; that it has something to do with what he really taught when He was here; that it will be shown to me when things are…ripe. It was odd how he paused and emphasized that word, as if it had some special meaning, or something. Anyway, the result will be the coming of heaven to earth. That just as each individual soul must go through its own resistance before it dies to its old ways, so, too, does humanity have to pass through to its next stage of growth."

"And what is that, exactly?"

"Universal Christ Mind, as natural as ego-mind is to humanity now."

It's Kendra's turn to walk over to the fire, where she sips slowly, very slowly, on her hot spiced wine. It shimmers on her lips in the firelight before her tongue carries the last drops inside.

"That all sounds too incredible for me."

"I know. I feel the same. It's beyond me, totally."

Kendra comes to stand in front of me, now smiling.

"But you know what isn't beyond you?"

"No, what?"

"Hawaii!"

"Oh, god! I nearly forgot! What time is it?"

She comes to me as I stand and steps into my arms.

"I think it's your time. That is what I think."

I slip my jacket on. At the door, I turn back to her. Kendra's smile softens my heart a bit.

"By the way, do you remember that book you loaned me some time ago, the one by a guy named Alan Cohen?

"Yes!" she replies. "Did you read it?"

"No. But, the other night Jeshua suggested—quite strongly—that Alan would be writing a foreword for the book. Can you imagine that? I don't know a thing about him!"

She clutches the blue binder fondly to her chest.

"Mind if I take care of this for a while?"

I nod a 'yes.' Had I known what this was soon to mean, the nod would have been a most emphatic 'no!'

After our eyes meet in silence for a moment, we share one more very long hug, and it's off to the airport.

Chapter Eleven

There are old friends waiting,

and I come with you

to call them to Myself

yet again.

Stepping out of the waiting area at the airport gate, I am hit by the sweet, delicious fragrances of Maui, the heart-island. Closing my eyes, I drink deeply with my breath this intoxicating scent. It's enough to bring a touch of tears to my eyes. Is it okay to consider an island your most precious of loves?

I step onto the escalator that takes me down toward baggage claim, then it will be onto the rental car bus, and then, and then, what? Why have I come here, really?

I am a patient sitting in the waiting room of the Grand Cosmic Doctor. My symptoms?

Hearing the voice of Jeshua.

Being shown images of events that haven't occurred.

Feeling compelled from a place in me that is beyond me to follow an unseen trail through a territory I never knew existed until I found myself in it!

Is there a pill for this?

Hunger! Thank God! I can always count on my appetite to serve as a needed distraction! There's a great little health food store not far from the airport, in Wailuku, called Down to Earth. And I could use a little of that!

⌒∞⌒

Having paid for my salad and carrot juice, I turn to head out the door, when my eyes catch a stack of magazines at the end of the counter. It looks like some sort of local thing, so I throw it into my bag, and head, where else? To the beach!

The sand is hot beneath my feet, and even the sound of the gentle surf rolling onto the shore seems soft. In fact, the whole island of Maui feels soft; as soft as velvet.

Having cleverly put on my swimming suit just before landing, I kick off my shorts, peel off my shirt, and run into the warm tropical ocean waters. I open my eyes to the sting of salt water, delighting in the endless visibility. Ribbons of sunlight dance downward toward a sandy bottom further and further away from me as I swim out, and out, out into this incredible, healing ocean.

Relaxing on my back, arms outstretched, I bob in the gentle, lapping waves one hundred yards offshore, gazing at dancing wisps of clouds in an endless blue sky. I can't contain a long, loud scream. This time, of utter ecstasy! At just that moment, my hunger returns with a vengeance. Turning over in the water, I look toward the distant shore, and beyond to majestic Haleakala, house of the sun, the mountain that really is East Maui, at whose sandy feet I will rest, and eat.

Gulping down the last of my carrot juice, my eyes rest on the thin magazine I picked up at the store. I start to absentmindedly thumb through it, occasionally noticing a short article here, ads for things like yoga, sufi dancing, and what-have-you. I am more than a little distracted from reading by a couple of remarkably attractive bikini-clad women baking in the sun, thankfully not all that far from me.

Sparkling, warm ocean to swim in. Great food. Jungles, waterfalls, hidden pools, and an extinct volcano. And bikinis. No wonder they call Hawaii 'paradise.'

"I could definitely live here," I mutter, forcing my eyes back to the magazine. "Maybe someday."

At just that moment I am drawn to a small ad at the base of the page. It's really the face I am drawn to, but why? What is this sudden jolt of energy in my spine? It isn't anyone I know, but I somehow know I need to know her. Next to her picture are simple words:

'Sara Patton. Wordsmith. Manuscript preparation, friendly support for authors.'

181

Chapter Eleven

In less than ten minutes, I have completed my call to her from a phone booth, and my appointment is set for tomorrow. I just know Sara will be the one to shape *The Jeshua Letters* into form. And I haven't even made it to my condominium yet!

❦

Sara is entirely focussed as she reads through page after page. I can't notice anything that tells me if she likes it or not. She turns pages a bit faster, so maybe she is losing interest. I'm sure that must be it. I knew it. This was just my fanciful mind playing tricks on me, again.

She stops on the last page. It's taking her way too long as I watch her eyes follow each line, then again, and yet again. The silence is palpable.

Finally, she looks up at me. Still reading, but not the manuscript.

"I would be honored to help you prepare this."

Did she really say that?

"You have had quite an experience. Is it still going on?" She closes the binder, and turns to place it on her desk. I recognize it is no longer in my hands. But then, was it ever?

"Well," I stammer a bit. "I mean, the manuscript is done, almost, but, no, I have a feeling things are just getting started."

Her warm smile relaxes me.

"It's okay. I work a lot with spiritually-based authors, so I can understand something about how this must be for you. But don't worry. If He chose you for this, He will handle things for you."

She seems nonchalant, matter-of-fact, and reassuring, all at the same time.

"In fact, I know who would love this, and it would be wonderful because maybe he would provide an endorsement for you!"

"Who are you talking about?" I ask her.

"Oh! Sorry, I just got really excited for some reason. Alan Cohen. Do you know his work? He lives right here on Maui. It would be easy to get him a copy of this!"

Jeeeeeeezzzzzzzuuuuussssss!

I can't help it. I start laughing a nervous laugh, and finally tell Sara about the 'prophecy' Jeshua had given me concerning Alan, this stranger I have never met, but—through Sara—will soon be reading **The Jeshua Letters**.

"Well, you see? Just as I said! If He chose you to bring this through, it looks like He is already a step ahead of you!"

Or, maybe a thousand. I wonder if I will ever catch up. I used to think my salvation was in becoming a know-it-all. But it is beginning to feel like the real direction is in becoming a trust-it-all!

My meeting ends with my signature on a contract, and Sarah's promise to get to work immediately. She will get the manuscript to Alan within the week, but just as I am leaving, she decides to give me his phone number.

"It feels like it would be best for you to call him, first."

And with that I leave Sara Patton, wordsmith, and drive away from her apartment in Maalaea, back along the road that runs next to Sugar Beach, back toward my condo in paradise, and toward something I am beginning to dread.

Soon, I will be calling a perfect stranger, and saying something like,

"Hi, there. You don't know me from Adam, but I have this manuscript. What's it about? Well, does the name 'Jeshua' mean anything to you? No? I didn't think so."

Egad! I have to tell a perfect stranger about this. It was one thing to let Sara read the manuscript. At least that gave me some distance! But now, I have to 'cold-call' a stranger, and 'fess up! Boy, do I need to take a nice, long swim. How far is it back to Tacoma, anyway?

❦

"Aloha! This is Alan!"

The voice is gentle, open, enthusiastic. And he doesn't even know who is calling yet. God, do even the people living here take on this soft Maui quality? Somehow, I stammer through introducing myself, letting Alan know Sara has referred me to him.

"Well, if Sara likes it, it must be good. She does great work, you know. You have been dropped into good hands!"

I wonder if he'll say that after I tell him by Whom! I begin to blurt it out. All of it. When done, I stop, and listen to my heart beating fast in the otherwise silent interlude.

In my mind's eye, I abruptly see an image of Alan, his eyes closed, as if praying about what I have told him. I also see Jeshua, standing near him, smiling at me. At just that moment, the inner image disappears, replaced by Alan's voice.

"Forgive me, but I felt the need to close my eyes and tune in to Spirit."

My mental image was a coincidence, I'm sure.

"Your manuscript feels good to me," he continues. "I would be happy to read it."

"Really?"

"Sure! I'll give Sara a call, and she can send over a copy to me. How long will you be on Maui?"

He's actually going to read it! "Uh, only another week. Unless, of course, I move here."

Move here! Of course! I mean, it's not like I have a job to get back to! Wow!

Alan laughs. "She's stealing your heart already, isn't she?"

"She?"

"Mother Maui! Somebody has to say 'yes' to their joy. Might as well join us!"

Saying 'yes' to joy? Really? Fully? Is that okay? Does it actually work?

⬿

My talk with Alan ends. I just couldn't quite bring myself to tell him one little piece. The bit about Jeshua saying he would write a foreword for the book. I mean, this is our first 'date,' after all!

After hanging up the phone, I walk outside and sit on the grass. It's nearing sunset time. The tradewinds are slacking off to a gentle caress. The sun is deliciously, almost erotically, exquisite on my face and arms. A cardinal lands on the grass, eyeing me for a bite of something.

"Sorry, friend. I have nothing to give you, unless you would happen to like some interesting bedtime reading!"

I show him my empty hands, he tilts his little head from side to side a few times, then flies off. The light is beginning to turn golden, like liquid gold shaping into rivulets as the sun nestles down behind the edge of the island of Lanai out on the horizon.

I look around….Maui. Live here, in all this beauty? Me? It dawns on me I can be broke here as easily as anywhere. And, after all, there is someone working on the manuscript. Maybe I ought to trust that. Yes! That is exactly what I am going to do!

Suddenly, as I look up at the stars, then the looming curve of Haleakala, and breathe in those amazing sweet scents, Mother Maui is seeming more and more like home.

Who am I kidding here, I think to myself. It felt like home the first time I came here back in 1973. The year I began meditation practice. Where I met my first Zen master. Maui is the comfortable pair of jeans I put in the closet and forgot about Why did I do that? Why wasn't I willing—or able—to let myself be where I love to be the most?

That thought strikes me hard. It is like a symbol of far deeper things, isn't it? After all, what has kept me all these years, all these lifetimes revealing themselves like fragments of a forgotten dream since Jeshua's appearance; what has kept me from opening to really receive the heart and soul of the Truth so obvious in His words? I have to know, to really and fully know, what that is all about! Not just for me, for all souls. Just what keeps the world spinning around as it does? What keeps suffering in place, like a broken record?

And in the snap of a finger, one key moment of my life explodes into awareness:

Vietnam. I am eighteen. The fire fight was horrific, sudden, deadly for too many. Now I stand digging yet another foxhole in yet another unknown spot in a never-ending jungle in the central highlands. Looking up, I am transfixed by the most beautiful sunset I have ever seen. Such beauty! Is it the shocking contrast of beauty and pain that does it? For I am being stretched to infinity, until the sunset is in me as much as I was just a moment ago looking at it. There is no end to me, all things are within me, and I pervade all things. Then, as suddenly as it began, I am again standing with shovel in hand. I notice it is dark. At least an hour must have passed! Why did no one disturb me? Awareness of the night, and the jungle sounds I have learned to hear so acutely in service to survival, returns. I jump down into my foxhole and look up at the few stars I can see through the canopy.

"What the hell was that? God, if there is such a thing, I have to know what that was! And, and what is this?—this insanity in the world, and this beauty. What the hell is going on, really? I have to know! Tell me, dammit!"

There is no reply and, in time, I am again a soldier in heightened alert against the danger out there, hidden in the jungle. A mosquito brings me back to the present. With a slap, I realize it just had its last moment of life. I'd forgotten that moment in Vietnam. It got buried under the deluge of the rest of that year, and of years since then.

❧

Maui is resting into the coming night, but the air is still so soft and sweet. Such beauty! I leap up to my feet.

"Well, that's that! It's cold in Tacoma! Hey, Mother Maui! Meet your newest resident!"

Opening the screen door to go inside, one simple thought arises:

Perhaps my soldier's prayer was heard, and—for Christ's sake—just maybe all of this, every moment since that night has all been part of the unfolding of the Answer.

It isn't just a thought in my head. It resounds from head to toe.

"Damn," I utter.

Undressing and laying on the bed—with no need to close windows or pull up the covers—I simply rest, feeling my breath rise and fall, learning bit-by-bit to be present with it as Jeshua has been instructing me, feeling it enter, not just into my lungs, but oozing in through every pour, streaming out as every tension dissolves into Light.

> ***Remember, my brother, to let God's love breathe you.***

Perhaps one day I will know what that really means. I no longer trust my intellect's understanding, the one thing I had always banked on! Perhaps He is right. On the road of a genuine spirituality, maybe there really is nothing to be gained. Only everything mistakenly accumulated to be lost, leaving room only for the Reality of God.

What would it mean, really, to submit to such a journey that many would think insane? Holding hands is one thing, making love another, but really surrendering to be ravished, to be utterly taken, well, that is another thing entirely. It feels like I have been invited to a party I grow more wary of, the closer I get, no matter how inviting the music!

I roll over on my stomach, eyes falling on the branches of night—blooming jasmine prancing gently in the breeze. If only I could surrender as easily as it seems to, to breezes unseen! It certainly doesn't seem to contract in fear, or wallow in complaints and confusion, nor demand how the breeze tosses it! It just seems to enjoy the dance.

I close my eyes. Right now, there is nothing to do. I live here now, and have no plan. Funny, but it doesn't seem to matter. Kendra will be surprised, but maybe not! There is nothing to do but get to know Maui better.

My attention turns toward Him, that ancient Friend out there in the ethers of reality, unseen by the eyes of the body, but not missed by the eyes of the heart:

Jeshua, if you want the book published, you are gonna have to do it yourself. I could make it happen, but what would that prove? I refuse to make anything happen with this! In fact, if you are who you say you are, you are going to have to prove it, and I mean, shatter every last doubt I have!

The energy of that thought is so strong it makes me sit up on the edge of the bed. "Whew, where did that come from?" I wonder.

I make my way to the shower, and stand beneath slightly cool waters, tumbling from forehead down across closed eyes, streaming to the drain at my feet. There's a strange feeling deep down in my belly, almost to my pubic bone. It's new, like I have just discovered some subtle room in my house I didn't know was there. How odd!

An image appears. It's a large trap door in a wooden floor. It appears right where the strange feeling is occurring. This time, I manage not to move away from it, but into it, putting into practice what He has been teaching me. To feel into the edge of resistance. He has said someday I will know that doing so is to be the presence of Love itself.

A soft whisper emerges from me: "I will trust you, Jeshua. All the way. There is no other way left now. No turning back to familiar ground. There is only one way to ever know what this strange, new territory with you is really all about."

The trap door opens, and the strange feeling increases. I feel like I am falling, or opening, or, well, I am not sure. My whole body feels different. Whatever the trap door has opened me to, now feels to be everywhere, in every cell. And the streaming water feels so wondrous!

His voice startles me. It comes from behind me, and I would swear I can feel the presence of Him standing behind me. But I don't turn to look.

Very well, My brother.
For this have I waited patiently longer
than you currently know.
There is much to set in place,
and we now commence
our chosen Work together.

Your only role is to allow Me to lead this,
until our purpose is completed.

Doubt will come, and go, and rise again.
Strive only to remember this moment,
and you will not again be defeated
as in an ancient past.

Now,
return to your Tacoma.
There are old friends waiting,
and I come with you to call them
to Myself yet again.

For the time is at hand.
All things will come to be remembered by you,
in due time.

Let your ancient faith in Me be restored,
and trusted until My promise to you is fulfilled,
and you are fully returned into the Father.

Trust, beloved brother, the love for Me you have
allowed to be rekindled.

Nothing else need be done, but this.

An invisible field of energy seems to release me. I turn off the shower, and return to the bed, where I lay quietly stunned for some time.

I think I have started a new job, but don't remember when I signed the contract! And I think union benefits are out of the question. But, for now, at least, the resistance is gone.

"So much for living on Maui." With that, I roll over, into a very deep, deep sleep.

⌒∞⌒

"You *w-h-a-t!!!???*"

My shock has exploded loudly, causing passersby in the airport corridor to turn and look, and the elderly lady at the phone next to me has dropped her coins in her coffee!

"Sorry, ma'am," I mutter apologetically. She moves to a different phone.

"Kendra, run that by me again. You say you gave the manuscript away? To a stranger?"

Kendra recounts her story, interrupted by my groans. Sighing, I try to shrug it off.

"Well, what's done is done. No, it's, it's okay. Guess if I am gonna do this trust thing. I don't get to pick and choose. Hey, my flights about to board. Yeah, bye."

We hang up and I saunter, slowly, toward my gate, half muttering to myself.

Kendra has handed my manuscript to a perfect stranger, saying only she felt a strong impulse to do so. No idea who, much less, why.

As I make my way onto the plane, the one that is carrying me away from this island I love and back to winter's cold in Tacoma simply because some part of me is choosing to heed a voice that comes from a being I can't even see. I recall watching episodes of Star Trek where they would suddenly lose control of the Enterprise, then a voice would boom over their speakers:

'You have entered the land of the Borgs. We are in complete control of your ship. Resistance is futile.'

Captain Kirk, I think I know how you must feel. Good bye, Maui.

Chapter Twelve

Trust, again, is essential.

It is also your final lesson

in the field of time.

March 15, 1989

"How are you doing?" Kendra asks.

I cradle the telephone handset between my left ear shoulder, and try to continue washing the dishes.

"I'm washing the dishes. Again."

"Again?"

"Yes, again. Too much nervous energy, I guess."

I stop and walk away from the sink.

"This is crazy, Kendra. In a few hours you and a small handful of friends will be here, and I don't have a clue what's going to happen!"

"What's the worse that can happen? It's just among friends, you know."

I lean against the wall. "But will they still be friends after this?"

Kendra laughs, but I don't.

"Look, I'll see you at seven. I gotta go downstairs to my office, close the door, and figure out how to deal with this, this, oh, hell, it's good ol' fashion fear, Kendra! And, by the way, thanks, for coming tonight."

"Didn't think I would miss it, did you? Just remember to come out."

"Out?"

"Of your office! See you later!"

With that, the phone call ends, and I descend the stairs to my office.

Closing the door gently, I take a deep breath. Usually I love coming to this small room in the home I found so quickly after returning from Maui. It's as quiet as a vault. But tonight it feels oppressive, as though the walls are closing in.

I step to the edge of my yoga map, and launch into a series of standing postures, noticing how difficult it is to stay present, and trying to get my breath deeper than my chest is like pulling teeth. It tells me from there down, I am contracted in fear; fear like thick concrete upon which my asanas are faint chisel blows.

Coming down to the mat face down, I begin to work harder. But it's no use. Finally, I just stretch out, still face down, and give up.

That is when I hear Him. No, first, I feel Him. Strongly.

More strongly than ever.

> *Hello, My brother.*
> *And so we begin to take the next step*
> *in an ancient Work shared before.*
> *You have again given Me your trust.*
> *I shall not leave you until all is done.*
>
> *Now,*
> *I ask that you open your Bible.*
> *Please begin reading in Jeremiah.*

Did I hear Him right? The Bible? I don't even know where the damn thing is. Jeremiah? For some bizarre reason, all I can think of is that old pop tune, 'Jeremiah was a bull frog.'

Rising from my mat, my eyes survey my bookcases. Hundreds and hundreds of books on philosophy, religions, physics, and what-have-you. I almost feel a disdain for them. For not one of them has helped me prepare for this strange journey with my unseen Visitor.

Scrounging about, I finally find it, buried beneath a stack of papers on a bottom shelf. For a moment, I recall how I deftly skirted anything to do with it during my university days.

I have to look in the index to find the page for the Book of Jeremiah. As I flip to it, the butterflies in my stomach kick it up a notch. Several, actually. Immediately, He speaks to me. God, His voice is so clear, that I can turn away and look out the window with no loss of connection, not unlike a friend talking to you while you attend to other things. Only I am unsuccessful at tuning this friend out!

Begin reading now.

I do so. As I reach the fifth verse, He stops me.

Please read out loud, slowly,
That you may truly hear,
For these are my words to you now.

Out loud. Slowly. Okay. I guess this is one of those moments that was sure to come when I said I would trust Him, after all.

"Before I formed you in the womb I knew you;
before you were born I sanctified you;
I have made you a prophet to the nations."

As I gasp, and feel that familiar nemesis strike hard and quick in my belly, He speaks again:

Now, read Verse Nine.

"And the Lord said to me: I shall put My words in thy mouth."

My mind, my breath, my body's movement are all slammed into stillness.

My brother,
I have chosen you because you first chose Me,
long ago.
I shall direct you to those whom I serve,
those who have called out to Me.

Fear not,
for do you truly believe
you can possibly prevent Me
from speaking to those I send to you,
or distort what I would share
as I continue My Father's will in service
of the Atonement of creation?

Again, I say unto you,
trust—together with your unceasing willingness—
is all that you need bring to our Work together.

It shall come to pass that, one day,
all will realize this is all that is ever needed
as miracles come to heal all suffering.

Heed not the voices of others,
but turn to Me,
and I am with you.

Trust, again, is essential.
It is also
Your final learning lesson
in the field of time.

Now,
The time is upon us.
Let us go,
and abide with those
who are now gathering.

Fear not, beloved brother.

Fear not.

∽

His energy fades. I become aware of muffled sounds above. Voices, laughter.

I hurry to scribe what just happened, and the words He spoke. I have a feeling they are going to remain etched in my brain as long as the thing keeps working.

Upstairs now, I am barely aware of the greetings as I move to sit in a chair in front of the half dozen or so friends, all staring at me, wondering what is about to happen.

Touching my index finger to my forehead, and gently stroking downward to the bridge of my nose, over and over, repeating a prayer He instructed me to do whenever we join in this way, I feel the world recede away in the distance. The body itself becomes soft, and softer still, until it, too, seems to disappear in a mist of light and color, as waves of bliss and peace engulf me.

It all gives way and I am aware only of Him, perceiving us together in an infinite field of purplish light.

> *All things are prepared,*
> *And now we will begin.*

This is when I notice we are not alone. There seems to be a host, a large circle, of beings, all shimmering in light. All within this field of purplish light. I can vaguely make out my living room, and the friends sitting, staring at me.

No! They are staring at my body, and so am I! Only, I am looking down on it. Jeshua moves to a place just behind it. He seems, then, to move into it. It is the last thing I am aware of, until it is all over.

> *Thank you, My brother.*

His voice startles me. Rapidly, I become aware of my body again. It's a rather rude experience. I open my eyes, but it takes several moments before everything settles into things; people, flowerpots, chairs, walls. But it's the people. Faces staring at me, eyes wide. Some with mouths open, all unmoving. They look stunned.

My body is vibrating, pulsating. Finally, I am able to speak, or should I say, stammer.

"Wh-what happened? There was this light and then..."

Silence. A long silence. No one has moved. Then, one by one, each rises. A few come to me and touch my leg, or my hand. But say nothing. In due time, everyone has left. I am still sitting in the chair, vibrating, pulsating in energy, with Kendra looking at me. That is when I notice the shining remains of tears on her cheeks. She speaks softly.

"He, He spoke. To each of us. One by one. Everything. Our lives. Lessons. Next steps, if we are willing. Things no one could know. His own life. I . . . I mean, no one said anything. We just listened. And it was palpable. You could cut it with a knife."

"What?" I manage to say.

"The, well, the presence, the, the love."

She finally rises from her chair.

"I think I'll go now."

I don't seem able yet to get up and walk about. My legs feel like jello. Strangers made of jello. Kendra hands me a letter.

"I almost forgot. I grabbed your mail on the way in. Habit."

I take the letter, and watch her leave. Whatever occurred, it has clearly struck her.

⌒∞⌒

Everything is still vibrating. If I didn't know better, I would think I just ate several hits of LSD, only its been years since I tried that, shortly after my return from Vietnam.

I open the letter.

> Dear Marc,
>
> You don't know me. A friend of yours handed me a manuscript some weeks ago, at a lecture in Seattle. I must tell you, first, that I have been praying to discover and know the real Jesus. I know it wasn't an accident she gave

your manuscript to me.

I cannot tell you what this means to me. There is no doubt my prayer has been answered.

And I am writing to ask you if you would be willing to let me pay to have this precious book published. It would be an honor to do so.

Sincerely,
J.R.

Now, my own tears begin to fall softly. I am alone, but have never felt less so. Suddenly, it hits me full force. The sign! I suddenly remember His words to me:

> **Soon, there comes a clear sign unto you of the Work**
> **in which you participate, the Work of the Son's**
> **atonement. When you clearly choose the active**
> **participation in this Work, there will be nothing**
> **which will not be provided.**

I guess He wasn't kidding. For the first time, I look at my watch. It's after midnight. Over five hours have passed! I finally rise, gingerly, but the vibration isn't abating.

Walking out through the kitchen, I open the door to the night. It is quiet. Stepping out onto the grass, I feel it. I mean, I really feel it. The apple tree seems more like liquid light than a solid thing. Even the bricks of the garage feel intimately charged with this liquid, vibrating light.

I walk down the steps to the street, and look up at the stars. Somehow, they feel more like they are inside me, than above me. I don't even notice the cold. Clearly, something has begun. I have entered my own version of Brave New World, to borrow the title of that book. I hope the 'brave' part stays with me to the end of it. That is, if there is an end to it.

Turning back toward home, His presence is welcomed with a new ease, as if I have somehow figured out how to answer this cosmic phone line.

It will be dawn before, finally, this body sleeps. And, strangely enough, what comes with it, or the possible dawns to come, matters no more.

All things have been made new.

Epilogue

In the classic American film, *The Wizard of Oz,* the main character, Dorothy, transported suddenly to a new world, spoke for the soul when she said to her small dog and faithful companion: "Toto, we're not in Kansas anymore!"

My experience, related in *The Jeshua Letters,* was much like Dorothy's. I still notice twinges of disbelief at times – it was as if I was swept up and deposited on a different planet! Of course, I *was* swept up, turned inside out, and deposited back on the very same planet, emerging as a radically different 'me' in the process.

The call of ceaseless surrender – no matter what – leaves no room for the mind to reasonably assess things, as it comes to release the one thing the small ego mind wants: control!

It seems as if it was yesterday when Jeshua gave me such a key statement of universal wisdom: "My brother, what would you control save that which you mistrust?" Every step on the path of healing, and every call to incarnate more of Christ Mind has required me to rest first in this Truth, learn to see the fear underneath my desire to control, and then surrender it and leap!

My mind still cannot fathom how all that has occurred in the last thirty-plus years was possible, unless, of course, it is true that God's Love does collapse the need for time…and that we are truly supported in our willingness to submit to the alchemy of the spiritual journey, so that we become conduits for what Jeshua calls in *The Aramaic Beatitudes,* 'God's new creations.'

We cannot experience these 'new creations' unless we surrender and become willing to engage our inner demons, learning more deeply how to become the Presence in which our deepest drives, fears, doubts, sense of unworthiness, and guilt are healed – unless we allow all of the structured ideas and perceptions we carry about ourselves, others, and life itself to be flushed up into awareness, there to be dissolved in a Love that far transcends the limits of 'reason.'

From *The Early Years* channelings, onto *The Christ Mind Trilogy*, the years of diving deep into, and creating with Him *The Living Practices*, discerning under Jeshua's guidance *The Aramaic Beatitudes*, living homeless, traveling the globe to share and learn from others (like you!), making eight pilgrimages to Israel and many other pilgrimages to sacred lands, ten years founding and living in an ashram in Bali, birthing The *Jewels of the Christ Mind* program and many other online courses, and so much more...Jeshua has led me throughout.

Could I have known any of this would unfold? Of course not! And, boy, did I ever put up a good fight attempting at times to resist every bit of it! And clearly, it was not "me" doing it. Rather, God was having His way with me, and I have learned from it all one crucial, essential, vital thing: we simply cannot unfold God's life for us, which is what our life really is. Only God can do this, and this life will unfold only when we have truly said "yes," when we have surrendered our need for control, and allow ourselves to BE unfolded – then, and only then.

The entire body of teachings that comprise *The Way of Mastery Pathway* are astounding in both depth and breadth. We remain free, however, to elect just how far along the steppingstones Jeshua has set before us we will walk at any time.

What I have seen now, very deeply in myself and in the journeys of the thousands I have been blessed to grow with (even when such growth seemed a torment for ego) has revealed for me this truth: together, we are the makers of the 'world,' which is a projection of fascinating 'frequencies' made by 'bending' Light into distortions, so that what we see, feel, and believe is the opposite of Reality. That is our remarkable creation, called by Him "the dream of separation." But separation does not – cannot – exist.

What, then, an astounding thing we have done, experiencing what cannot exist! And still, Love calls us home, and however real the dream may seem, still, only Love is real. Indeed, the dream exists only in what we project upon reality, veiling the shimmering, extraordinary, infinite, and astounding Presence of God from ourselves, then using our creations in an attempt to regain what we threw away without having to remove those veils!

While only loving thoughts are real, until we heal beyond thoughts themselves and come to rest in the field of Love itself, often our 'loving thoughts' merely veil what remains to be healed into wholeness; we are hallucinating, still lost in the dream. And yet, Love is shimmering and smiling at us through all that we see, and we can come to see this Love infinitely, if we choose to. The "problem," then, isn't out there, it is with the nature of the seer. Turn within, then, not to escape, but to discern the veils that color reality, bringing all to Love for healing and correction.

Once we do this, we no longer hold onto the belief that, "If I just 'wake up,' I can finally escape this damn world," because we no longer have a desire to escape.

Waking proves that we have been utterly wrong about awakening itself, for the result is just the opposite – it is not about escaping at all but about embracing and loving our 'enemies.' For as we are free to choose what we put our attention on, and thereby create our experience, we see that our true 'enemies' are merely the veils we have allowed to cloak our minds, express through our bodies, and warp our very use of life and time.

That even thought arises from a far more primary field of energy, of frequencies made of Light that can veil Light from operating not just as thought, but as feeling, as the true power and potential of Love— this profound realization is what sets the fullness of *The Way of Mastery Pathway* apart from most forms of spirituality.

We are 'the world.' And it changes only as we choose to change. Until we become conduits for the transfiguring power of Love exactly where we have thought we were trapped – like Dorothy in Oz – there is no completion in Christed Being.

As these realizations truly began to dawn for me as a result of my journey under His masterful guidance, Jeshua led me to a statement in *A Course In Miracles* that I had not heard anyone teaching the *Course* refer to, let alone emphasize: "Heaven and earth will pass away means only they will cease to exist as separate states." Yes. There is no room for the hope of getting 'beamed up,' or shirking total commitment to our own transformation and serving the healing of all, nor can we justify ongoing distraction (which most of the world is designed to be – just go shopping!) if our deeper desire is awakening to Truth, Love, and Reality!

Jeshua makes it clear: "Christ assumes responsibility for the whole of Creation."

The Christ Path is one of radical death to self, rebirth, *and* a call to see that 'there is no other, you see only your Self,' a call to fully participate in the very process of coming to experience heaven and earth as ceasing to exist as separate states.

All we need do is humbly, fully, devotedly, allow Love to guide our own unique journey from fear to Love, under all conditions. All the rest will unfold from there, exactly as the creations of 'my life' have unfolded from the willingness to be 'taken all the way, no matter what.'

The Way of Mastery Pathway is a vital part of such an unfoldment for many, and though we may never meet face to face, we journey on it together, and I want you to know I am grateful for each time you choose forgiveness, or are willing to look within and question the little mind, open to new revelations, and are moved to new creations and choices to extend Love to one and all.

What Jeshua says is true: "This we do together, until all of Creation is returned to being only the praise of God's Presence." Peace comes when, truly, this is seen and known, and we see that the bringing of fear to Love, and the bringing of illusion to Truth for healing and transformation, for seeing the remarkable, joyful journey that this includes, is the only truly worthwhile use of time.

Blessings to you!

Jayem
July 2021

The Way of Mastery Outline
Pathway of Enlightenment

The book you hold in your hands is part of a larger body of work, namely *The Way of Mastery*.

The Way of Mastery is a pathway offering a profound and comprehensive theology and lived experience of love via a progression of teachings, exercises, and *Living Practices*, all devoted to a genuine – and radical – depth of living enlightenment.

This depth goes beyond intellectual belief or the acceptance of certain concepts and ideas. It guides the student into their essential and eternal Heart, into a radical, transfigured gnosis, a 'knowledge by being that which is known.'

The purpose of *The Way of Mastery Pathway* is threefold:

~ To create a pathway that can support any student from their first steps all the way to truly awakening into 'Christ Mind'

~ To restore the original Teachings of Jeshua (Jesus) given to His followers

~ To 'birth a million Christs'

The Way of Mastery Pathway is comprised of four essential and interconnected parts:

~ **The Jeshua Channelings:** *The Jeshua Letters, The Early Years, The Way of the Servant, The Christ Mind Trilogy: The Way of the Heart, The Way of Transformation and The Way of Knowing and The Later Years.*

~ **The Living Practices**: a series of alchemical trainings and Aramaic teachings, including *LovesBreath, In the Name* meditation, *The Aramaic Lord's Prayer, The Aramaic Beatitudes, Radical Inquiry,* the seamless life and more.

~ **Facilitated Teachings and Sacred Journeys:** deepening into a spiritual path often requires support; private sessions, workshops, seminars, on-line classes, sacred pilgrimages and a host of classes and gatherings are led by *Pathway* teachers.

~ **Temple Canyon Sanctuary:** sacred land near Abiquiu, New Mexico, miraculously purchased in the early days of the Pathway, and meant for future steps of development, as given specifically by Jeshua during the time of its purchase.

∽

In summary, *The Way of Mastery* is a Pathway of Enlightenment that re-establishes Jeshua's original teachings, and in doing so, it offers a profound, in-depth roadmap to support any soul from the first inkling to awaken all the way into knowing their most essential Self.

The *Pathway* aims at nothing less than a radical shift of identity from 'Ego' to 'Christ,' aiding students to increasingly live in and create from Christ Mind, itself. Through His *Pathway*, Jeshua seeks nothing less than the birthing of "a million Christs" on this planet and the transformation of the experience of humanity from fear to Love— the manifestation of Heaven on Earth that 'completes the very need for Time.'

Jayem is the channel of *The Way of Mastery.*

Official Website: www.wayofmastery.com

Shanti Christo

'Shanti Christo' is a term mentioned often in *The Way of Mastery* texts. The meaning of Shanti Christo is 'Peace of Christ.' This term was first given by Jeshua to Jayem prior to the unfolding of the *Pathway* (as *The Way of Mastery Pathway* is often called) itself.

Shanti Christo was also the name given to the non-profit foundation that Jayem set up in the early years of his channeling with Jeshua. The Shanti Christo Foundation was established to disseminate *The Way of Mastery* teachings, and to steward the Temple Canyon Sanctuary land near Abiquiu, New Mexico, until time for it to be developed further.

In 2002, Jayem received guidance from the Holy Spirit related to the foundation and his role within it. Following this guidance, he resigned as its director and continued his own deep immersion with Jeshua. It feels important to share the portions of the guidance related to Jayem's role for you to read directly:

> *"First, you* [referring to Jayem] *must step aside completely. You have successfully completed the stage of vision. The twofold purpose of the entity* [Shanti Christo] *is fully revealed and given: the teachings, which began with* The Jeshua Letters *and ended with the three works entitled* The Way of the Heart, Transformation, and Knowing. *Second, the physical setting has been attracted, discovered, purchased, and its design features openly shared* [the land near Abiquiu].
>
> *"The next stage, implementation, is not your role or your concern.* [Jayem interjects at the time of the channeling: 'And frankly, this is a surprise to me in big doses.' The reading continues:] *Remember, you can only be what your Creator would make of you, not what you may perceive you should be."*

Holy Spirit later goes on to share:

> *"Your only role* [speaking directly to Jayem], *the essence of your existence, is to bridge vision and the teachings of Christ mind to others, thus fully learning them yourself."* ★

As a result of Jayem's continued immersion with Jeshua, further stages of the *Pathway* developed after his departure from the foundation – namely the *Living Practices* (*Love'sBreath* and *Radical Inquiry*) and *Facilitated Teachings*. Also included in this unfolding was what Jeshua states as a primary purpose of the *Pathway*: "to restore My original teachings." These unfolded under His guidance and are known as the *Aramaic Teachings*, which in themselves express the soul, depth, and heart of the entire *Pathway*.

Interestingly, this development was 'predicted' in Lesson 10 of *The Way of Knowing*. Jeshua revealed that much more would be coming forth after the completion of what came to be known as *The Christ Mind Trilogy*:

"…as we enter these last days of this *Way of Knowing*, we have come in this hour to share with you that we do not so much come to a culmination, or an end, but to a *springboard* for what shall be."

To this day, Jayem continues to develop teaching tools that provide valuable assistance to thousands as they engage *The Way of Mastery Pathway*. He has gone on to become a masterful facilitator and continues his dedicated servantship with Jeshua – holding His vision for the *Pathway* as sacred.

⌒∞⌒

Notably, after Jayem stepped away from the Shanti Christo Foundation, its board elected to publish only three of the five core teachings: *The Way of the Heart, The Way of Transformation,* and *The Way of Knowing*. Substantial sections of these texts were edited and removed, including the questions and answers that followed many lessons, and the trilogy was published within a single book entitled *The Way of Mastery* (referred to by many as the "blue book").

While this publication served to disseminate the teachings to many, identifying the trilogy under this title has also created confusion for many students who have come to equate *The Way of Mastery* with a single book. The *Pathway* is far from complete without *The Jeshua Letters* and *The Way of the Servant* texts (which the Shanti Christo Foundation chose not to publish), and the crucial experiential components that Jayem has continued to develop—*The Living Practices, Facilitated Teachings,* and *Aramaic Teachings.*

⌇

This series of books—the only authorized and complete version now in print—has been published to ensure that students understand the broader context in which *The Jeshua Letters, The Way of the Servant,* and *The Christ Mind Trilogy* were given, and that they are only one part of a comprehensive 'pathway that can carry anyone from the first inkling to awaken all the way to Christ mind.'

May *Shanti Christo*—the Peace of Christ—be with you.

* *The complete text of the 2002 Message is available on our website:* *wayofmastery.com*

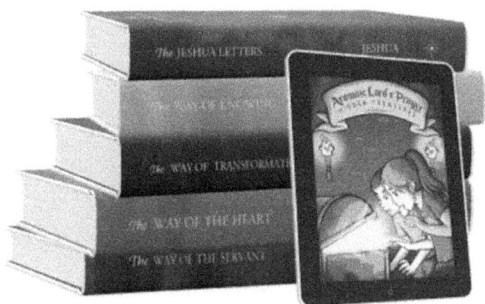

Way of Mastery Pathway

The *Way of Mastery Pathway* offers a comprehensive road map if you have the desire to **grow,** to **heal** and to **know yourself**.

Find out more about what is available by visiting our website: www.wayofmastery.com

WAY *of* MASTERY
w w w . w a y o f m a s t e r y . c o m